KOCHER VIADUCT
CHARLES BRIDGE
KHAJU BRIDGE
BRIDGE
DANYANG–KUNSHAN
GRAND BRIDGE
VICTORIA FALLS BRIDGE
LIVING ROOT BRIDGES
CHRISTMAS ISLAND
CRAB BRIDGE
SYDNEY HARBOUR BRIDGE
KAWARAU BRIDGE

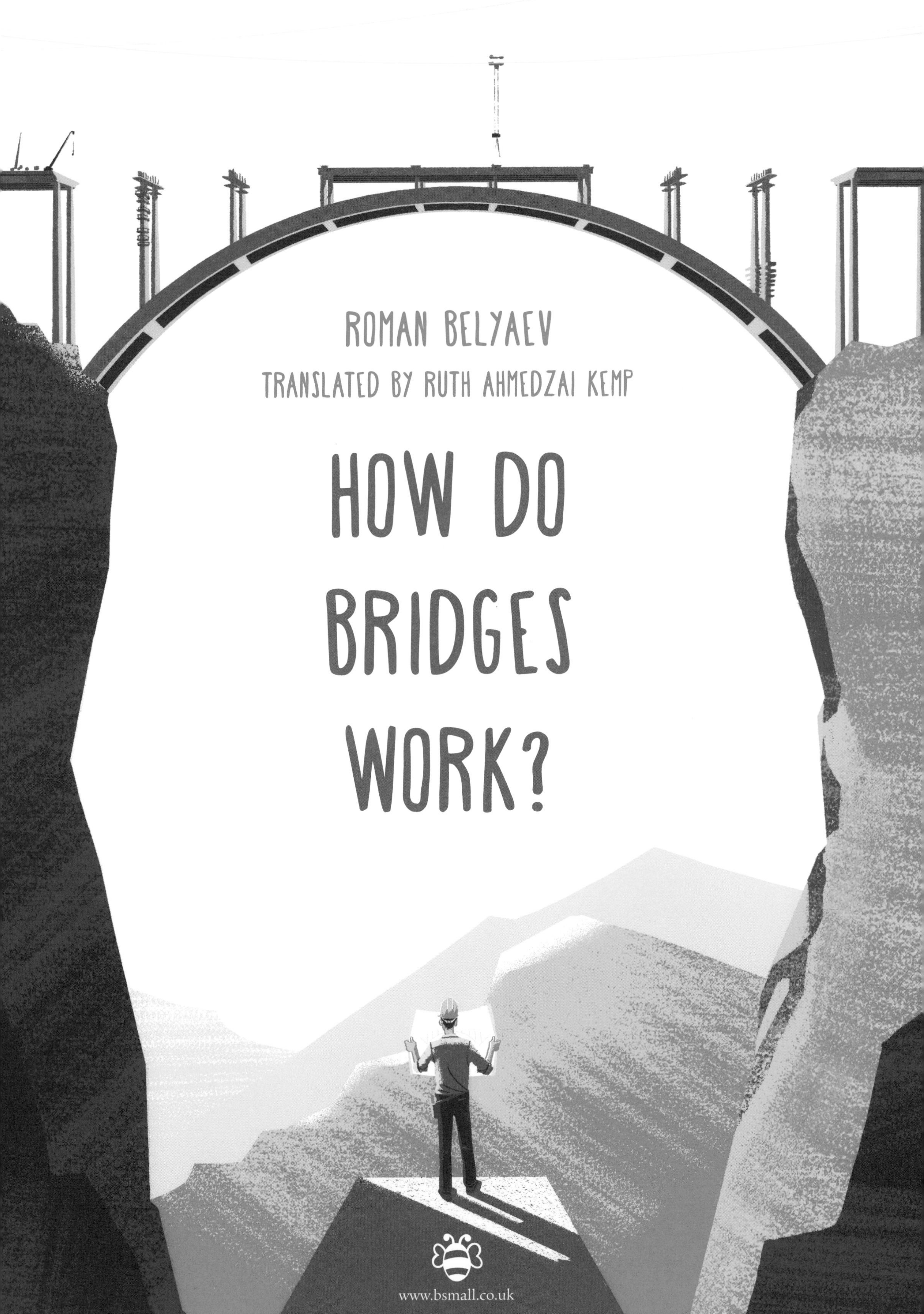

ROMAN BELYAEV

TRANSLATED BY RUTH AHMEDZAI KEMP

HOW DO BRIDGES WORK?

www.bsmall.co.uk

THE FIRST MAN-MADE BRIDGES APPEARED ON THE PATHS CREATED BY ANCIENT FARMING COMMUNITIES.
IN ANCIENT ROME, ROADS AND BRIDGES WERE A MODE OF COMMUNICATION: MESSENGERS SPREAD NEWS AND MERCHANTS SPREAD RUMOURS.

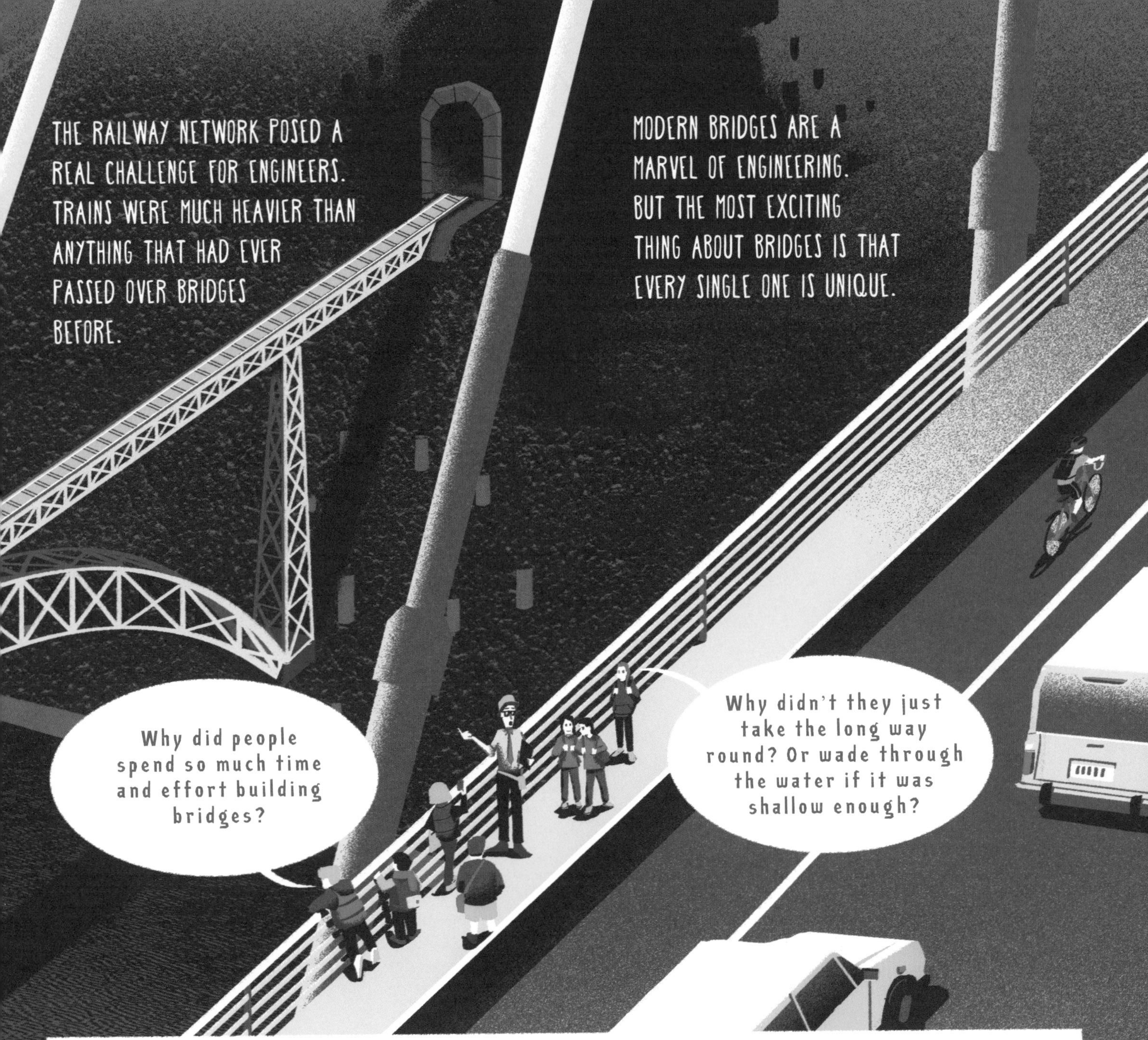

WHY WERE BRIDGES INVENTED?

Nomadic tribes did not build bridges. They were constantly on the move and had no need for permanent structures. But the first ancient kingdoms and states needed bridges to help their armies move around easily and for messengers to take decrees, or laws, to the people. In the Middle Ages, wealthy cities built wide bridges over rivers to improve access to their markets and attract even more merchants. Then, with the invention of railways and cars, bridges became an essential part of modern transport networks. Today we travel effortlessly across gorges, rivers and even seas, and we rarely stop to consider that each bridge is a unique solution to a difficult technical problem. Let's have a look at what bridges are and how different they can be.

WHAT DID THE FIRST BRIDGES LOOK LIKE?

The answer to this question depends on what we mean by the first bridges. Do we mean ways of crossing a river that emerged naturally, like a fallen tree? After all, animals would have been crossing rivers like this long before humans came along. Or do we mean structures built intentionally by people? Yes, in this book we're talking about structures designed and built by people. But, unfortunately, we will never know exactly what the very first man-made bridge looked like. Before the advent of modern technology, most bridges were unreliable structures that needed constant work to maintain them. Sometimes they were temporary constructions that only lasted for one season, until they were washed away by a swollen river or swept away by storms. Because of this, all we know of bridges in ancient times is what we can learn from the few structures that survive to this day.

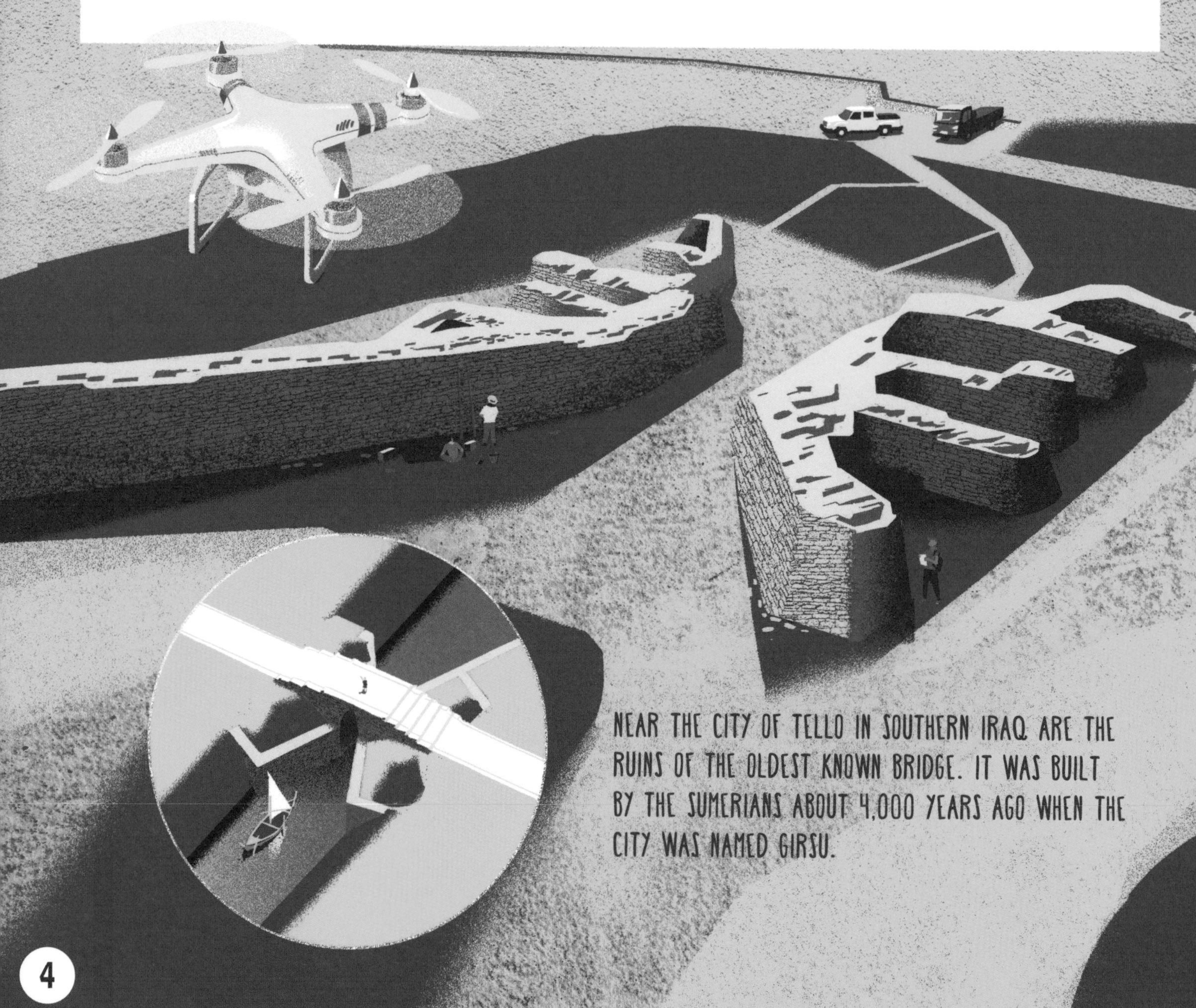

NEAR THE CITY OF TELLO IN SOUTHERN IRAQ ARE THE RUINS OF THE OLDEST KNOWN BRIDGE. IT WAS BUILT BY THE SUMERIANS ABOUT 4,000 YEARS AGO WHEN THE CITY WAS NAMED GIRSU.

There are several bridges that have a strong claim to being the world's oldest existing bridge. In fact, all these ancient bridges have been repaired and rebuilt so many times that it is impossible to determine the exact date of construction.

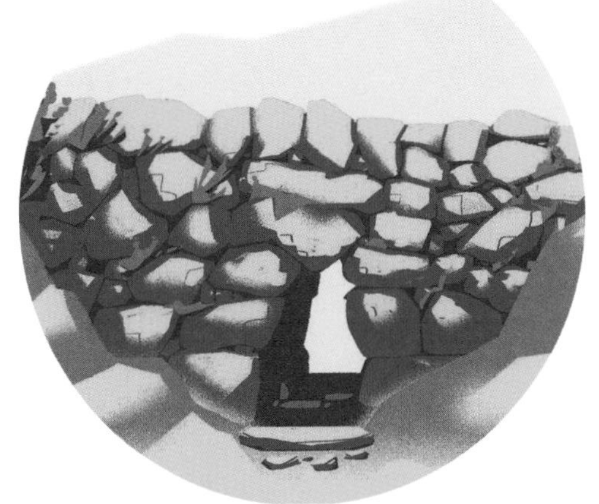

ARKADIKO BRIDGE (GREECE)

This is an ancient corbel arch bridge near Arkadiko in the Peloponnese. It is thought that it was built by the ancient Greeks around 1300–1190 BC.

TARR STEPS (ENGLAND)

This is a clapper bridge, formed from large stone slabs, across the River Barle in Somerset. It is unclear exactly when it was constructed. It was certainly there in the fifteenth century but it could date back to the Bronze Age. Over the centuries, the bridge has been destroyed many times by floods, but has been rebuilt again and again.

CARAVAN BRIDGE (TURKEY)

This is an arch bridge across the River Meles in Izmir, a strategic city for merchants on the Silk Road in the sixteenth century. Certain sources suggest that the bridge was constructed in 850 BC.

WHAT DO WE MEAN BY A 'BRIDGE'?

Bridges have been around for such a long time that the words we used to describe them come from early proto-languages, which are the ancestors of the languages spoken nowadays. For example, the English word *bridge*, German *Brücke*, Swedish and Danish *bro*, Norwegian *bru* and Icelandic *brú* all come from a word in the Proto-Indo-European language meaning 'wooden floor'. Another Proto-Indo-European word meaning 'road' or 'path' evolved into the Greek word *póntos* and the Latin *pōns*. The words for 'bridge' in French *(pont)*, Italian *(ponte)* and other Romance languages all come from these roots. The common word for bridge is *most* in all Slavic languages, but linguists are still debating the etymology (the origin) of this word.

GERMANY

THREE COUNTRIES BRIDGE

Not far from the Swiss town of Basel, the Three Countries Bridge spans the Rhine, where it forms the border between France and Germany. The river is 250 metres (820 feet) wide at this point and the arch bridge connects the French town of Huningue and German town of Weil-am-Rhein. The border of the third country, Switzerland, is just 200 metres (656 feet) south of the bridge.

WHAT ARE THE DIFFERENT TYPES OF BRIDGE?

Bridges vary enormously. The form of construction depends on whether the bridge is for pedestrians, road traffic or a railway, the physical geography of the area and the materials available, such as wood, concrete or stone. There are a few basic bridge forms that we will look at in more detail.

BEAM BRIDGE

This is the most common form of bridge. The span – the distance between two supports – is made up of one beam or deck.

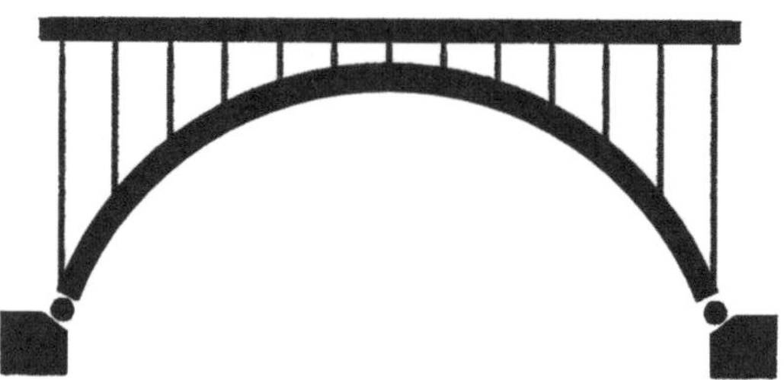

ARCH BRIDGE

This bridge design is considered the most reliable. Almost all of the ancient bridges that have survived to modern times are arch bridges.

SUSPENSION BRIDGE

The deck is held up by two main cables, stretched through supporting towers and anchored to the banks on both sides. The span is suspended from these cables, which are attached to the vertical towers. Suspension bridges can be built across wide obstacles where it would be impossible to build additional piers.

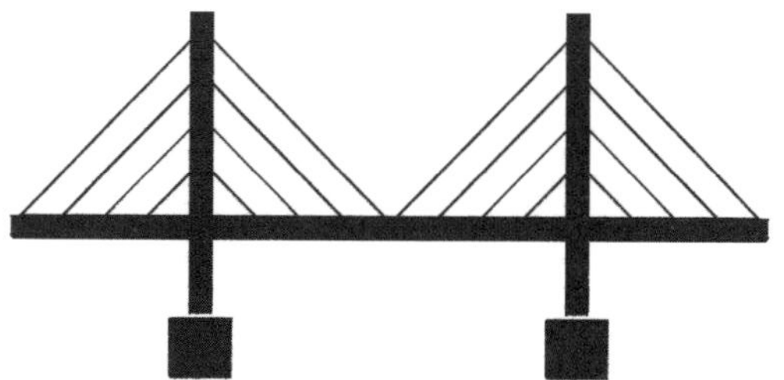

CABLE-STAYED BRIDGE

The span is held up by cables, which are fixed directly to the towers. There is the harp design (pictured), where the cables are attached to the supports at regular intervals, and the fan design, where all the cables are fixed at one point.

BEAM BRIDGE

ARCH BRIDGE

SUSPENSION BRIDGE

CABLE-STAYED BRIDGE

THE WORLD'S FIRST BEAM BRIDGES WERE MADE FROM THE TRUNKS OF FALLEN TREES.

– THE DIFFERENT TYPES OF BRIDGE –

BEAM BRIDGE

This is probably the first type of bridge constructed by people. In its most primitive form, a beam bridge is simply a log or stone slab resting on two supports or surfaces. Although relatively straightforward to build, the downsides of such bridges are that the beam can buckle under its own weight, so the maximum span length depends on the properties of the building material used. Modern high-strength materials mean beam bridges can be built with a span of nearly 80 metres (262 feet). But there is no limit to the number of spans used one after the other, which is why the world's longest bridge, featured on page 42, is a beam bridge.

KOCHER VIADUCT (GERMANY)

A viaduct is a bridge that crosses land rather than water, traversing obstacles such as uneven terrain. The Kocher Viaduct is part of the motorway, or Autobahn, between Heilbronn and Nuremberg. At 185 metres (606 feet), it is the tallest viaduct in Germany.

THERE IS A SMALL RIVER AT THE BOTTOM, BUT THE VALLEY IS SO BROAD AND DEEP THAT A SIMPLE BRIDGE WOULD NOT HAVE BEEN ENOUGH.

– THE DIFFERENT TYPES OF BRIDGE –

NATURAL ARCHES

Because of its graceful shape, it is most likely that the arch bridge design emerged originally from nature. Almost all types of rock, but especially sandstone and limestone, can be eroded by water and wind to form wonderful arch structures.

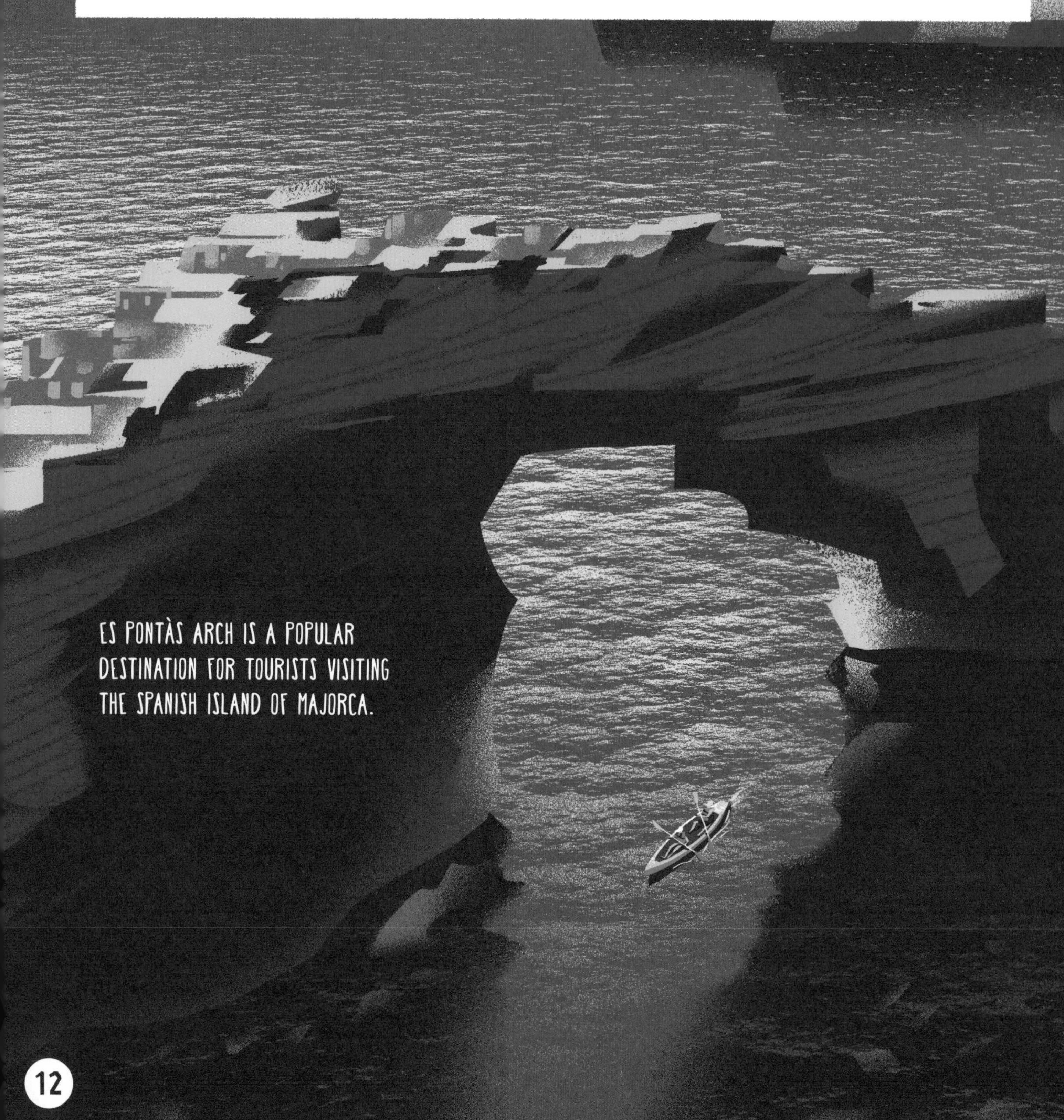

ES PONTÀS ARCH IS A POPULAR DESTINATION FOR TOURISTS VISITING THE SPANISH ISLAND OF MAJORCA.

ARCH BRIDGES OF ANTIQUITY

PONT DU GARD (FRANCE)

This ancient Roman aqueduct is 50 metres (164 feet) high and over 275 metres (902 feet) long.

Arched structures were being built as long ago as in ancient Mesopotamia. But the real revolution in construction came in the Roman era. Ancient Romans introduced the widespread use of waterproof concrete made with volcanic ash. It was thanks to Roman concrete that complex structures such as arches and domed roofs could become so widespread. Many ancient Roman buildings have not only survived to this day, but are still being used for their intended purpose. Water flows along aqueducts and people cross bridges that are over a thousand years old.

KEYSTONE (OR CAPSTONE)

A wedge-shaped stone that closes the top of the arch. It is inserted last of all.

CENTRING

A wooden frame that supports the arch until construction is complete.

VOUSSOIRS

Each wedge-shaped block presses against the ones it touches. As a result, the structure is strengthened by its own weight.

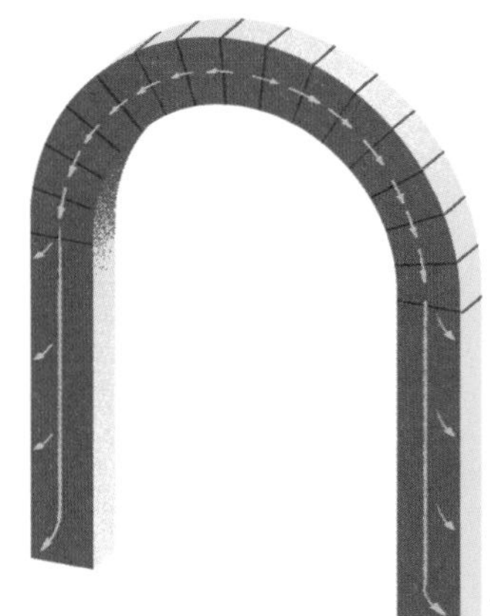

HORIZONTAL THRUST

This is the force pushing the arch outwards at the base. The sides of the arch need to be held in place firmly by an opposing force to prevent the arch from collapsing.

– THE DIFFERENT TYPES OF BRIDGE –

MODERN ARCH BRIDGES

Modern arch bridges can be up to 600 metres (1,968 feet) in length. This form of bridge is very reliable, but is not easy to build. Nowadays, the arch is usually delivered to the construction site as one ready-made piece or in several large pieces. How heavy a bridge can be depends on the points of contact between the arch and the ground as the arch will naturally flatten without an opposing force to push against. For this reason, heavier arch bridges need particularly sturdy foundations at either end of the arch. Although a basic arch bridge is easy to spot, as everyone knows the shape of an arch, in fact arch bridges can have very varied shapes and designs, depending on where the road deck sits relative to the arch.

ARCH BRIDGE STRUCTURES

The road deck crosses the top of the arch.

The road deck passes through the middle of the arch.

The road deck is at the bottom of the arch.

THE HOOVER DAM IS PART
OF A HYDROELECTRIC POWER
STATION BUILT IN 1939 ON THE
COLORADO RIVER.
THE FOUNDATIONS OF THE ARCH ARE
SET INTO THE ROCK. THIS ALLOWS
IT TO WITHSTAND THE ENORMOUS
STRAIN ON THE ARCH SPAN.

MIKE O'CALLAGHAN–PAT TILLMAN MEMORIAL BRIDGE (USA)

The first reinforced concrete arch bridge in the United States was finished in 2010 to bypass the busy road over the Hoover Dam, at the border of the states of Colorado and Arizona. At 323 metres (1,059 feet), this is the longest concrete arch in the Americas and it rises 270 metres (885 feet) above the Colorado River.

– THE DIFFERENT TYPES OF BRIDGE –

TRADITIONAL SUSPENSION BRIDGES

The first suspension bridges appeared in the highlands of Asia and South America. At first, these were made from just a pair of ropes woven from reeds, hemp or leather. To cross to the other side, you would shuffle along the lower rope while holding on to the upper one. Later, bridge builders improved the design by adding a wooden walkway. Suspended bridges began to look like the rope bridges we know from adventure films.

IN THE MOUNTAINS OF PERU, LOCALS WEAVE ROPES FOR THE BRIDGE FROM THE STEMS OF MOUNTAIN PLANTS.
THINNER THREADS ARE WOVEN INTO THICK ROPES.

LLAMAS ARE OFTEN USED TO TRANSPORT HEAVY LOADS IN THE PERUVIAN ANDES.
Perú
THE ROPES ARE PULLED ACROSS TO THE OTHER SIDE.
THEY ARE TIED TOGETHER FIRMLY AND WOODEN BOARDS ARE FIXED ACROSS THE BOTTOM ROPES.

– THE DIFFERENT TYPES OF BRIDGE –

MODERN SUSPENSION BRIDGES

The first suspension bridges that could withstand heavy transport were built over two hundred years ago. Over two centuries, ropes and chains were replaced by cables of high-strength steel or carbon fibre. The distance between the supports can now reach over a kilometre (3,280 feet). The design principle has not changed in all this time: a suspension bridge is always a span hanging from two flexible ropes. Suspension bridges allow us to overcome the broadest obstacles without the need for supporting piers along the way.

THE BRIDGE'S COLOUR HAS A SPECIAL NAME: 'INTERNATIONAL ORANGE'. THE PAINT PROTECTS THE BRIDGE FROM DAMAGING SALT SPRAY AND MAKES SURE IT IS ALWAYS VISIBLE, EVEN IN THICK FOG.

EACH LOAD-BEARING CABLE HAS A DIAMETER OF 92 CENTIMETRES (36 INCHES) AND IS WOVEN FROM 27,572 STEEL WIRES.

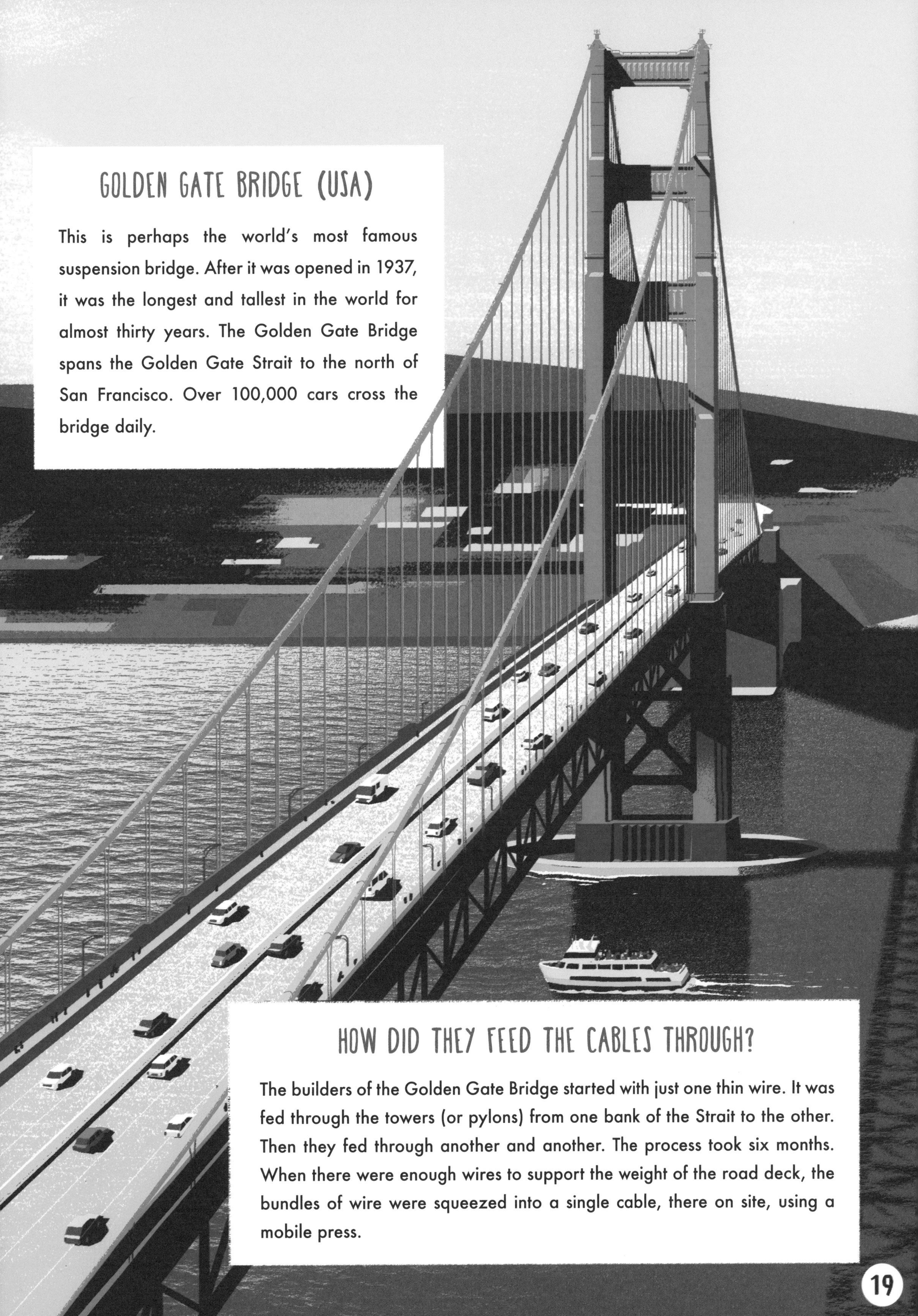

GOLDEN GATE BRIDGE (USA)

This is perhaps the world's most famous suspension bridge. After it was opened in 1937, it was the longest and tallest in the world for almost thirty years. The Golden Gate Bridge spans the Golden Gate Strait to the north of San Francisco. Over 100,000 cars cross the bridge daily.

HOW DID THEY FEED THE CABLES THROUGH?

The builders of the Golden Gate Bridge started with just one thin wire. It was fed through the towers (or pylons) from one bank of the Strait to the other. Then they fed through another and another. The process took six months. When there were enough wires to support the weight of the road deck, the bundles of wire were squeezed into a single cable, there on site, using a mobile press.

– THE DIFFERENT TYPES OF BRIDGE –

CABLE-STAYED BRIDGES

'Cable-stayed' means supported, or stayed, by thick wires, or cables. This is similar to the way the masts of sailing boats are held up by wires called 'stays'. The first cable-stayed bridges were built only 60 years ago. Bridges of this design are usually between 300 and 600 metres (984 and 1,968 feet) in length, but a cable-stayed bridge span can be as long as a kilometre. The harp design is where the supporting cables are fixed to the towers at regular intervals, whereas with the fan design all the cables are fixed at one point at the top.

'HARP' DESIGN

'FAN' DESIGN

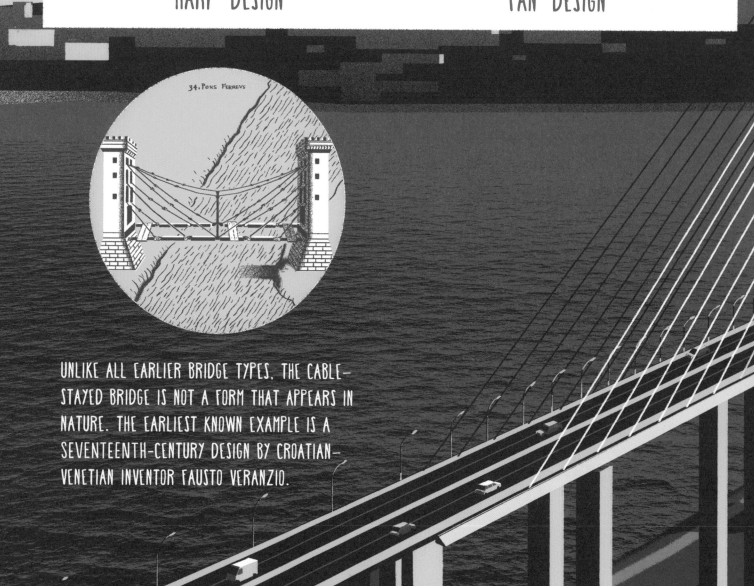

UNLIKE ALL EARLIER BRIDGE TYPES, THE CABLE-STAYED BRIDGE IS NOT A FORM THAT APPEARS IN NATURE. THE EARLIEST KNOWN EXAMPLE IS A SEVENTEENTH-CENTURY DESIGN BY CROATIAN-VENETIAN INVENTOR FAUSTO VERANZIO.

THE CABLES OF THIS RUSSIAN BRIDGE ARE PAINTED WHITE, BLUE AND RED – THE COLOURS OF THE RUSSIAN FLAG.

RUSSKY BRIDGE (RUSSIA)

Crossing the Eastern Bosphorus Strait at Vladivostok to the Russian island of Russky ('Russian'), this bridge is enormous with pylons 321 metres (1,053 feet) tall. The cables of this harp-design bridge support the world's longest span among cable-stayed structures: 1,104 metres (3,622 feet).

MILLENNIUM BRIDGE (ENGLAND)

Opened in 2001, this bicycle and pedestrian bridge across the River Tyne in the north-east of England was the world's first tilt bridge. Its arch was assembled on land and then installed on its supports using a floating crane. It is the seventh bridge to link the cities of Gateshead and Newcastle. The unusual parade of bridges, all built since the mid-nineteenth century, is popular with tourists.

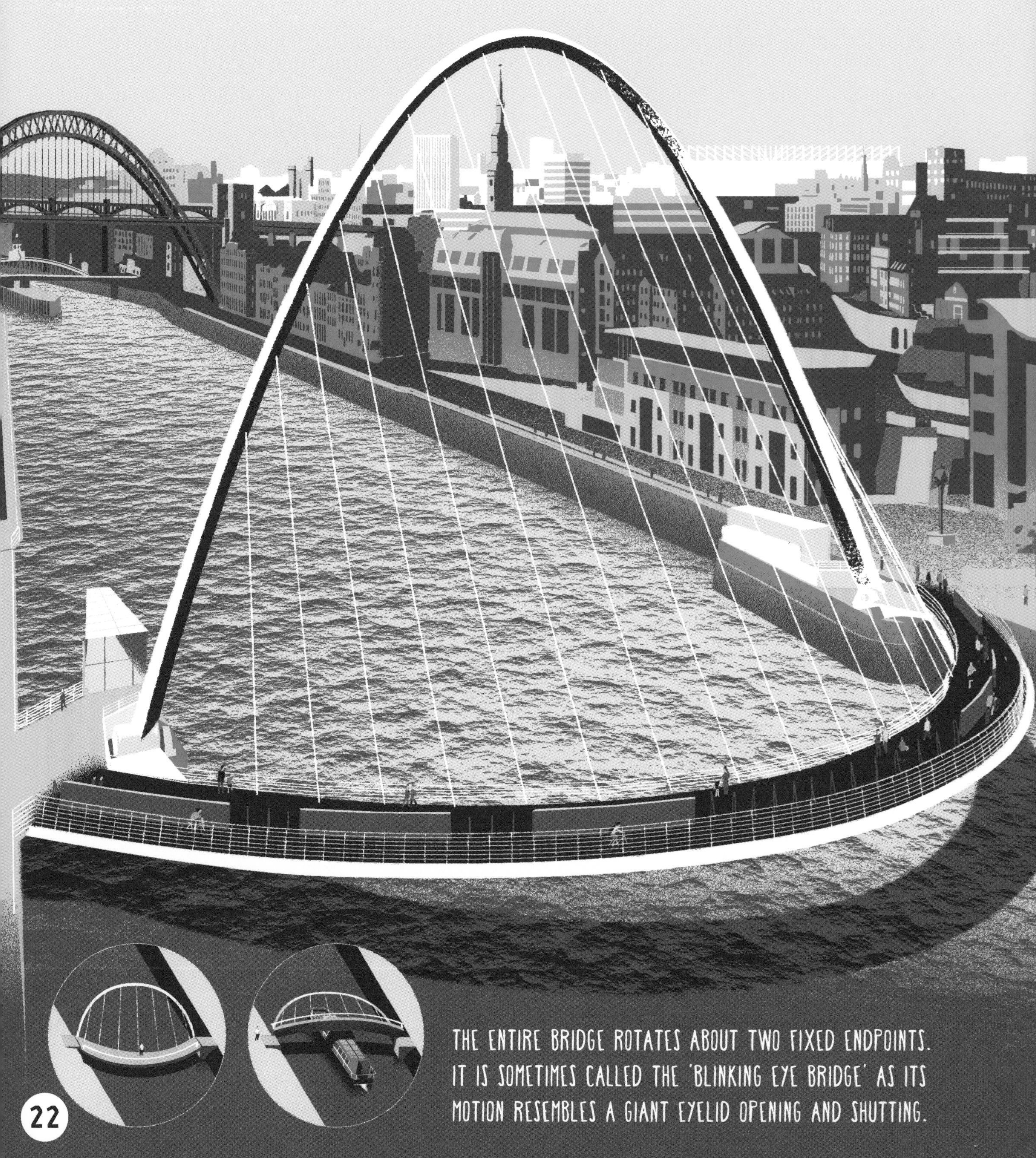

THE ENTIRE BRIDGE ROTATES ABOUT TWO FIXED ENDPOINTS. IT IS SOMETIMES CALLED THE 'BLINKING EYE BRIDGE' AS ITS MOTION RESEMBLES A GIANT EYELID OPENING AND SHUTTING.

DRAWBRIDGES

A drawbridge is not one design of bridge but rather a broad category covering many types of moving bridges. The key feature is that part of the bridge or the entire span can move, to make way for ships, for example. The first were those over castle moats, but the most common nowadays are bascule bridges, or movable bridges that are commonly referred to as drawbridges.

PONTA DA BANDEIRA FORT (PORTUGAL)

A drawbridge guards the entrance to this sixteenth-century fortress, built to protect the city of Lagos from marauding pirates. However, such bridges were known much earlier. It is believed they were in use in ancient Egypt.

PALACE BRIDGE (RUSSIA)

This bascule bridge is the most famous type of drawbridge or movable bridge. This design has been widely used since the mid-nineteenth century. Palace Bridge, an iconic sight in St. Petersburg, was opened in 1916.

VIZCAYA BRIDGE (SPAIN)

This is no mere bridge, but an entire transport system: a transporter bridge. Suspended from the bridge is a gondola or 'flying ferry' that transports passengers and vehicles from one riverbank to another, near Bilbao.

CORINTH CANAL SUBMERSIBLE BRIDGES (GREECE)

A submersible bridge is one where the deck does not rise, but instead is lowered beneath the water to allow ships to pass. The two bridges across the Corinth Canal sink to a depth of eight metres (26 feet).

HOW ARE BRIDGES BUILT?

In the Middle Ages, many bridges were dubbed the 'Devil's Bridge'. In an era when the Romans' secrets were forgotten, the construction of bridges became such a rare event that people suspected bridge builders of being aided by evil spirits, as in the case of the legend surrounding the construction of a bridge in the French town of Saint-Cado.

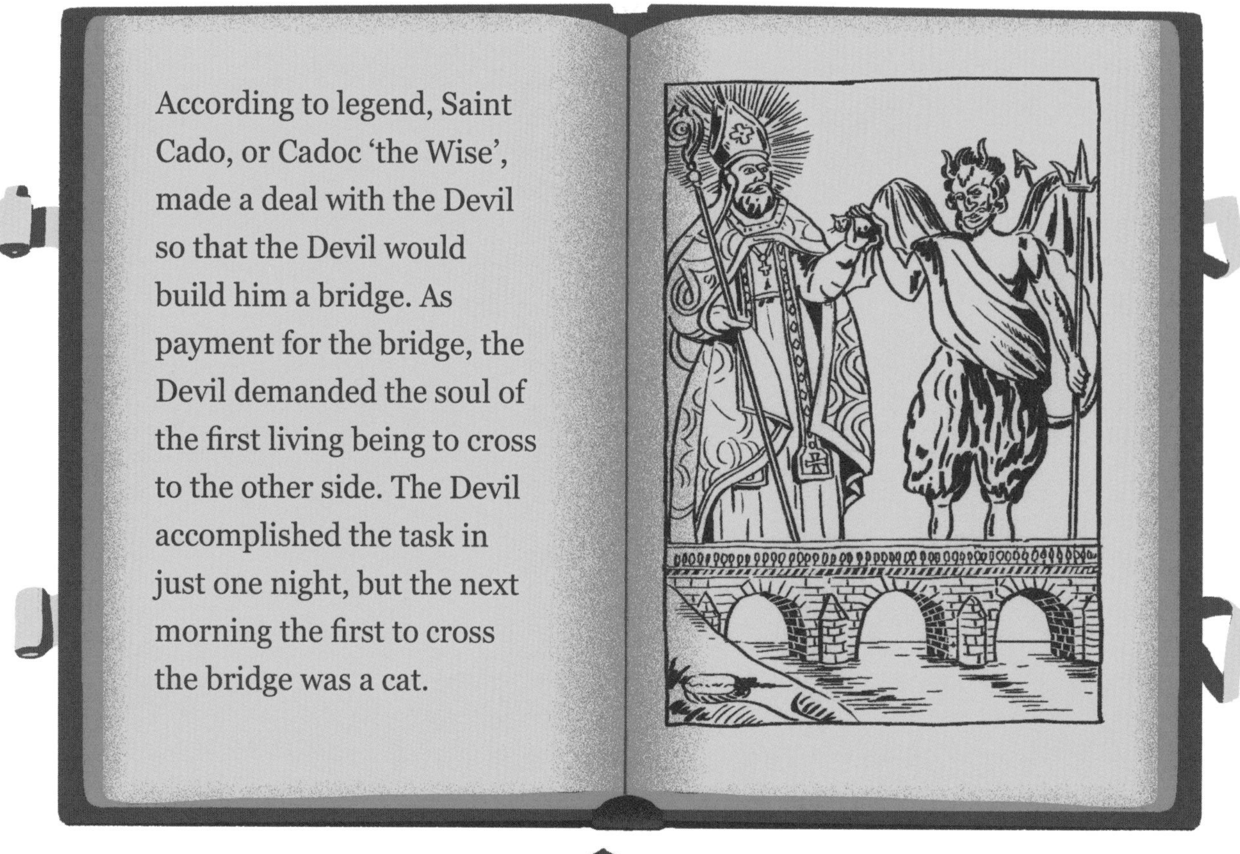

According to legend, Saint Cado, or Cadoc 'the Wise', made a deal with the Devil so that the Devil would build him a bridge. As payment for the bridge, the Devil demanded the soul of the first living being to cross to the other side. The Devil accomplished the task in just one night, but the next morning the first to cross the bridge was a cat.

Today, the construction of a bridge is still a difficult task, since each bridge has unique requirements. But, like any other project, it can be broken down into several standard steps. To begin with, the construction team needs to gather and analyse as much information as possible about the location where the bridge is to be built. They study the composition of the soil and rock, the depth of the water and the speed of the current. Then comes the design and planning stage. Only after that can construction begin. This also happens in several stages: first, they prepare the site and access roads, then they erect the bridge piers that will hold the bridge up and, when they are in position, the spans are laid on top linking the piers.

– HOW ARE BRIDGES BUILT? –

ERECTING THE PIERS

Whatever a bridge is made of, the materials stretch and compress under the influence of weight and changes in temperature. To allow for this movement, there are supporting parts between the deck and the piers below: these might be flexible supports to allow the span structure to move, or fixed supports to prevent movement.

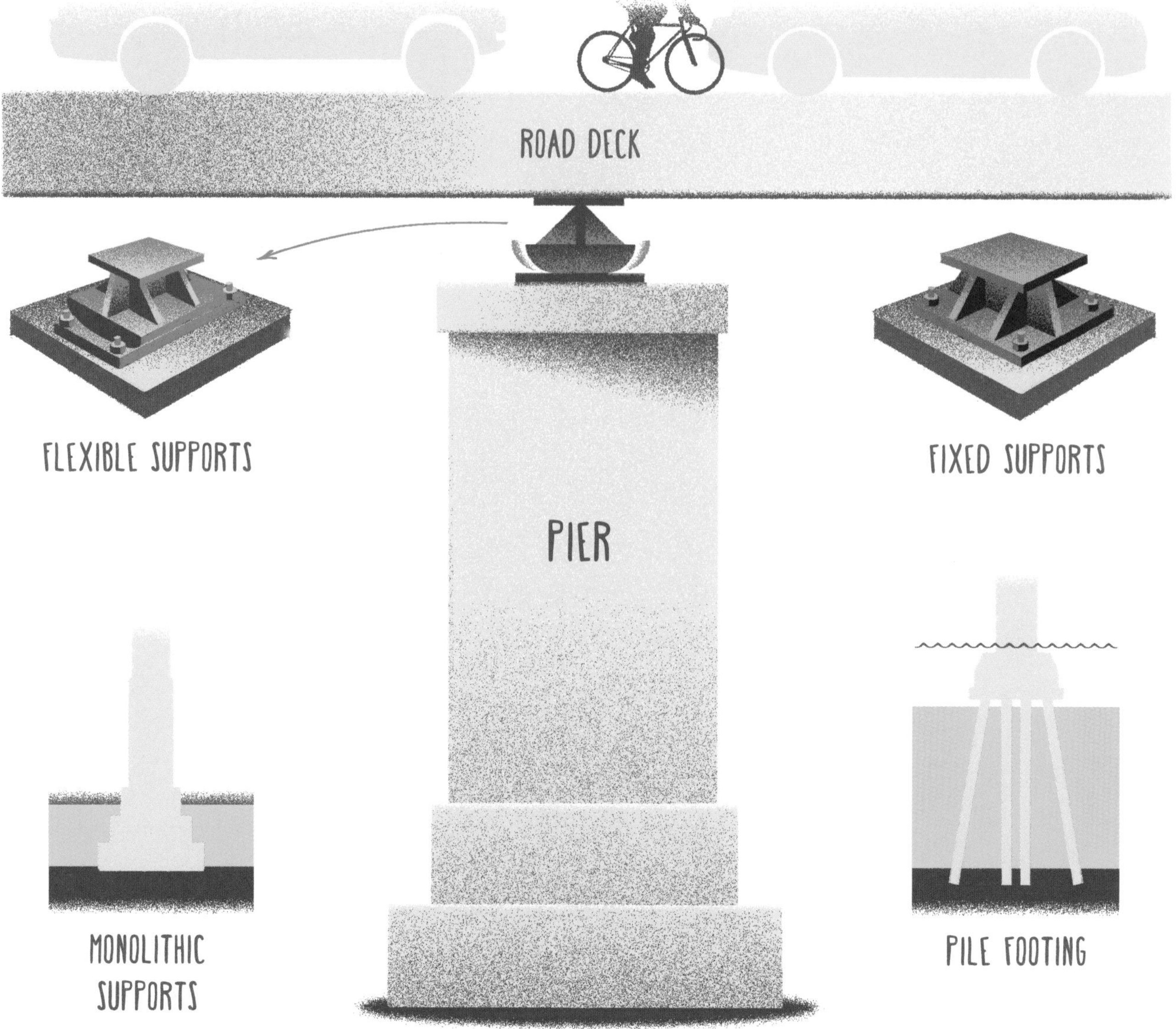

For the supporting piers to be as reliable as possible, they need a firm footing: solid foundations set into the ground. The engineers need to carry out a thorough analysis of the soil and bedrock before they decide what kind of footing to use. Sometimes you do not need to drill very deeply for a firm foundation, whereas in other conditions the footings need to be very deep.

BUILDING PIERS UNDER WATER

Various technologies are used to construct piers under water. Here are just a few of them:

SHEET PILE ENCLOSURE

If a future construction site is situated in relatively shallow water, engineers fence off an area using sheets of metal, pump out the water and then work in the same way as they do on dry land.

ARTIFICIAL ISLAND

If the bridge is to be built over deeper water, the place where the pier is to be set into the ground is covered with soil to form an island. The construction work then continues on dry land.

CAISSON

If engineers need to work at great depths, they use a caisson – a special water-tight chamber that is assembled on shore, towed to the construction site and sunk below the water to ground level.

TYPES OF SUBSTRUCTURE

There are many different bridge designs but there are only two types of supporting substructures: abutments and piers. Abutments are the supports at the far ends of the bridge, and piers are the supports spaced out along the length of the bridge.

ABUTMENTS

PIERS

This elegant arch bridge, built in 1911 in the centre of Rome, rests on abutments and piers.

VICTOR EMMANUEL II BRIDGE (ITALY)

The bridge is named after the first king of united Italy, Victor Emmanuel II. The piers are decorated with sculptures celebrating the unification of italy.

BUILDING THE ROAD DECK

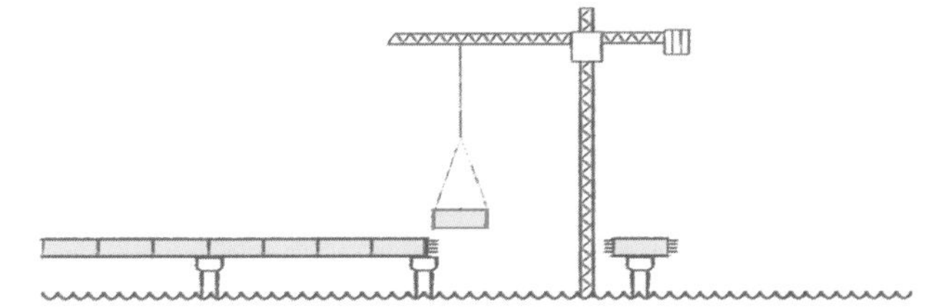

PREFABRICATED SECTIONS

Sections of the bridge deck are made in a factory and assembled on site using a crane or gantry. This is one of the fastest ways to build a bridge, but spans constructed in this way cannot be longer than 50 metres (164 feet).

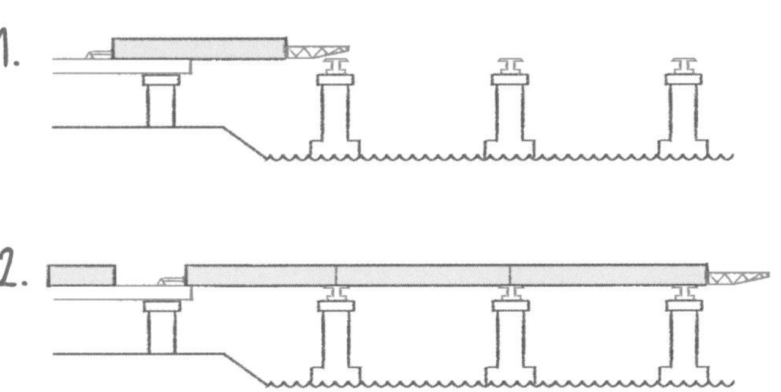

SLIDE METHOD

The spans are constructed on shore and then slid along to their intended position on the supporting piers. Sticking out from the concrete span you can see a lightweight steel structure. This is an example of a launching girder, which directs the heavy spans into position and stops them from slipping and falling.

CONSTRUCTING A CABLE-STAYED BRIDGE

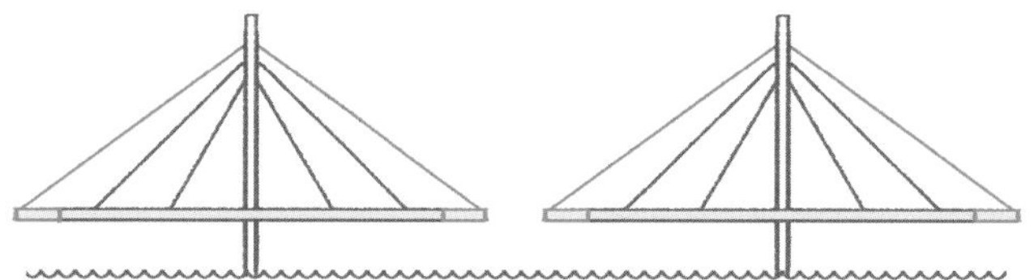

First the piers are installed, then sections of the deck are attached on both sides, for balance, and these are fastened to the tower with cables.

The central section is lowered into place using a big crane.

ARCH BRIDGE

ASSEMBLING AN ARCH FROM SEGMENTS

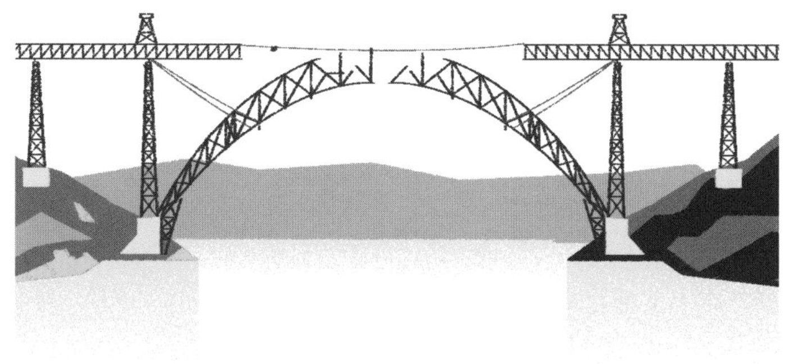

TOWING AN ASSEMBLED ARCH

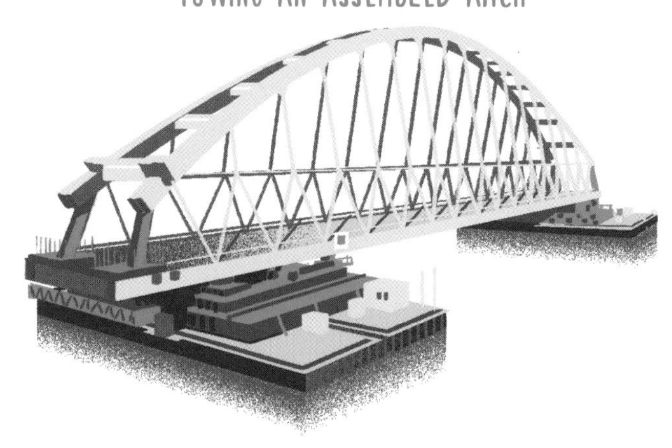

Before bridges were made of steel and reinforced concrete, the only available technology for arch construction was a temporary semicircular frame called a centre or centring, to hold the bridge segments, or voussoirs, in place until the keystone is inserted.

Today, arched spans are delivered to the construction site in several segments or pre-assembled arches are towed into position on the water.

FAMOUS BRIDGE BUILDERS

APOLLODORUS OF DAMASCUS

Apollodorus was a Greek engineer from Roman Syria. One of the most renowned builders of his time, he was the official architect at the court of the Roman emperor Trajan and built the Trajan Bridge across the Danube. At 1,135 metres (3,723 feet) in length, the bridge stood for less than 200 years, but it would remain unbeaten for another 1,000 years as the longest bridge in history. A wooden arch bridge with twenty stone piers, it was erected in AD 105 near the present-day town of Drobeta-Turnu Severin, on the border of Romania and Serbia. Trajan's Bridge was used as a military crossing and was demolished by Trajan's successor to prevent enemy invasions.

JOHN ROEBLING

Engineer and inventor John Roebling was famous as a designer of suspension bridges, of which the most renowned was Brooklyn Bridge, opened in New York in 1883. At his wire rope factory, Roebling improved the method for weaving steel wire into rope. These wire ropes were lighter and stronger than the chains used until this time. This new technology meant significantly bigger suspension bridges could now span longer distances and withstand heavier loads.

GUSTAVE EIFFEL

Gustave Eiffel is an engineer known primarily for his iconic tower erected in Paris for the international exhibition of 1889 and subsequently named in his honour. But Eiffel was also architect of many other civil engineering projects around the world, including bridges, railway stations and even the metal internal structure of the Statue of Liberty. His 1877 arched bridge over the River Douro, dedicated to Dona Maria Pia, is one of two famous bridges built by Eiffel in Porto, Portugal, that attract tourists to the city.

SANTIAGO CALATRAVA

The architect Santiago Calatrava Valls began his career in the 1980s. His architecture and engineering company has already built some 30 bridges. Their futuristic constructions, resembling sea shells or the skeletons of fantastic creatures, can be seen in major cities throughout the world. The Samuel Beckett Bridge, a cable-stayed bridge stretching 124 metres (406 feet) across Dublin's River Liffey, opened in 2009. Its shape is intended to recall the harp, the national symbol of Ireland.

THE MOST UNUSUAL BRIDGES

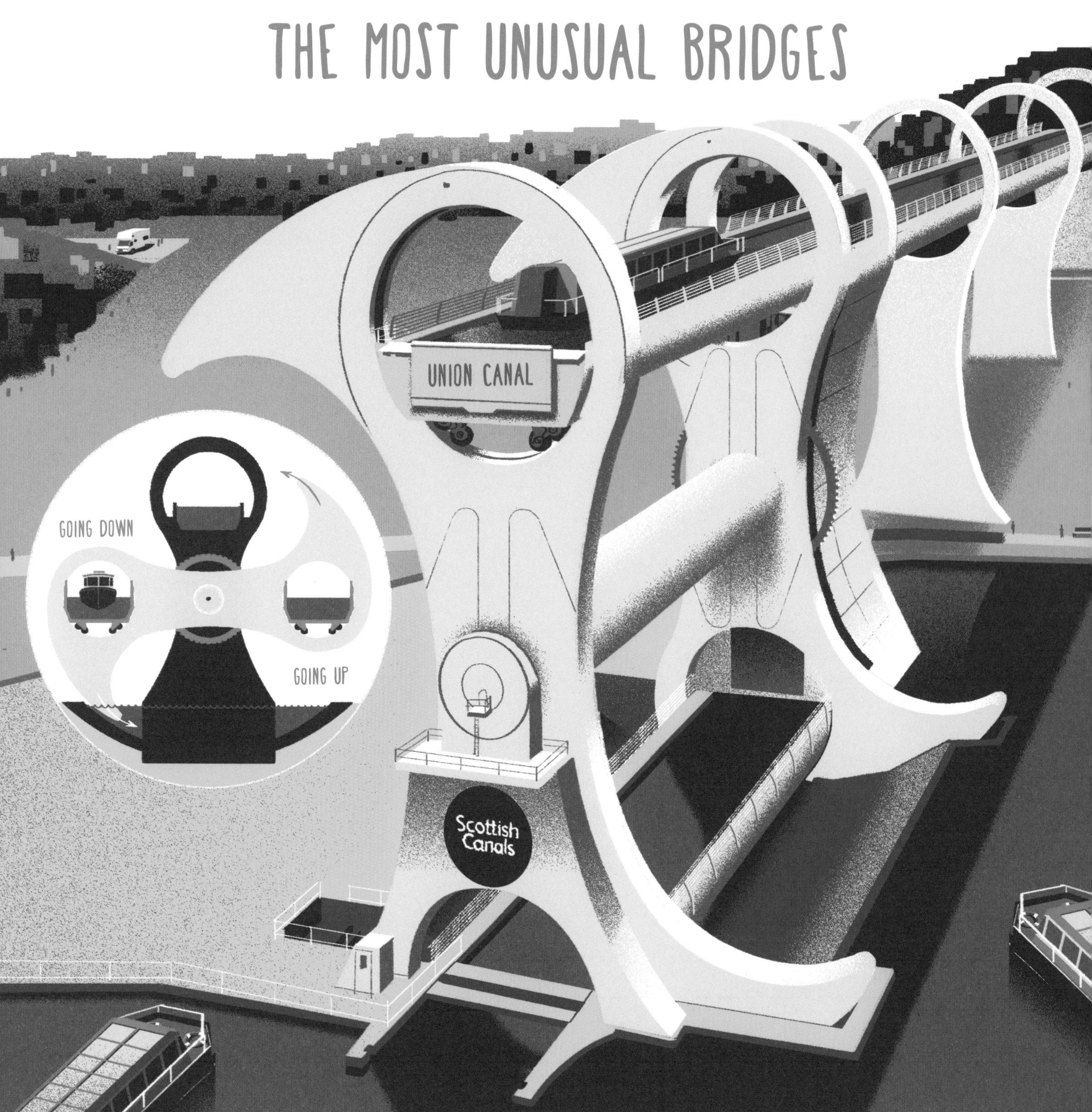

FALKIRK WHEEL (SCOTLAND)

This is the world's only rotating boat lift. The bridge connects two canals in Scotland, near the town of Falkirk. The design looks a little like a fairground Ferris wheel, only instead of cabins it has two special chambers filled with water, one on each side of the wheel. When the giant wheel rotates, the two chambers switch places, moving one boat up and another down through a height of 24 metres (78 feet) in four minutes. Before it opened in 2002, it would take an entire day to go up the flight of locks between the canals.

KAWARAU BRIDGE (NEW ZEALAND)

In 1988, the world's first bungy jumping site was opened in the South Island of New Zealand, on this suspension bridge, 43 metres (141 feet) above the Kawarau River.

THE BRIDGE OF SIGHS (ITALY)

This medieval bridge in Venice was completed in 1603, connecting the Doge's Palace, where the courtroom was located, with the prison. Legend has it that convicts would sigh as they took one final glance at Venice through the barred windows.

MOSES BRIDGE (THE NETHERLANDS)

This unusual bridge was built in 2010. It crosses the moat to a seventeenth-century fort. The architects designed the bridge so that it was set below the water level, making as little impact as possible on the historical landscape.

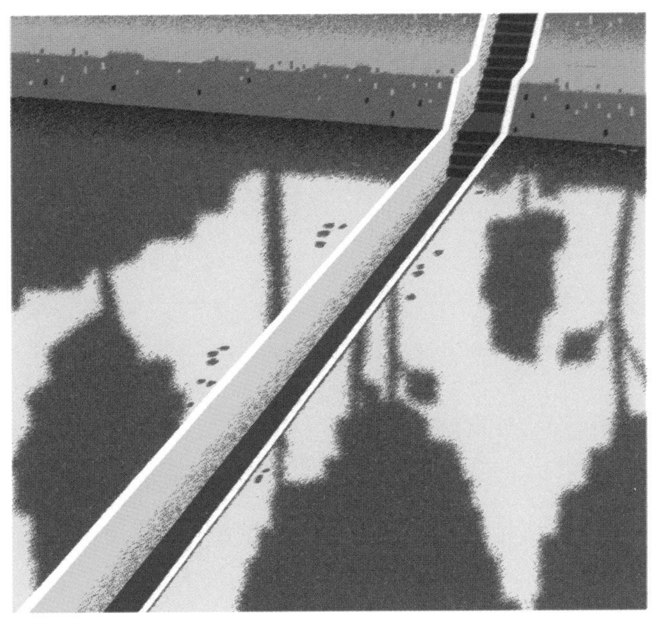

BLUE BRIDGE (RUSSIA)

One contender for the widest bridge in the world is thought to be the Blue Bridge in St. Petersburg. Its width is far greater than its length. Spanning the River Moika with a length of only 29 metres (95 feet), it is some 97 metres (318 feet) wide and is painted a bright sky blue.

CRAB BRIDGE (CHRISTMAS ISLAND)

In places where busy roads intersect with animal trails, people have created man-made crossings for the animals, sometimes referred to as 'ecoducts'. On Christmas Island, an Australian island near Indonesia, a bridge was built in 2015 to provide a safe migration route for red crabs.

LIVING ROOT BRIDGES (INDIA)

The forests near the Indian town of Sohra (also known as Cherrapunji) are famous for their bridges made of living tree roots. Builders lay a bamboo or wooden scaffold across the river, and the rest of the work is done by the roots of the rubber trees (*ficus elastica*) growing along the banks. The roots gradually wrap themselves around the canes and reach the opposite bank in ten to fifteen years. Some of these bridges have been in use for several centuries.

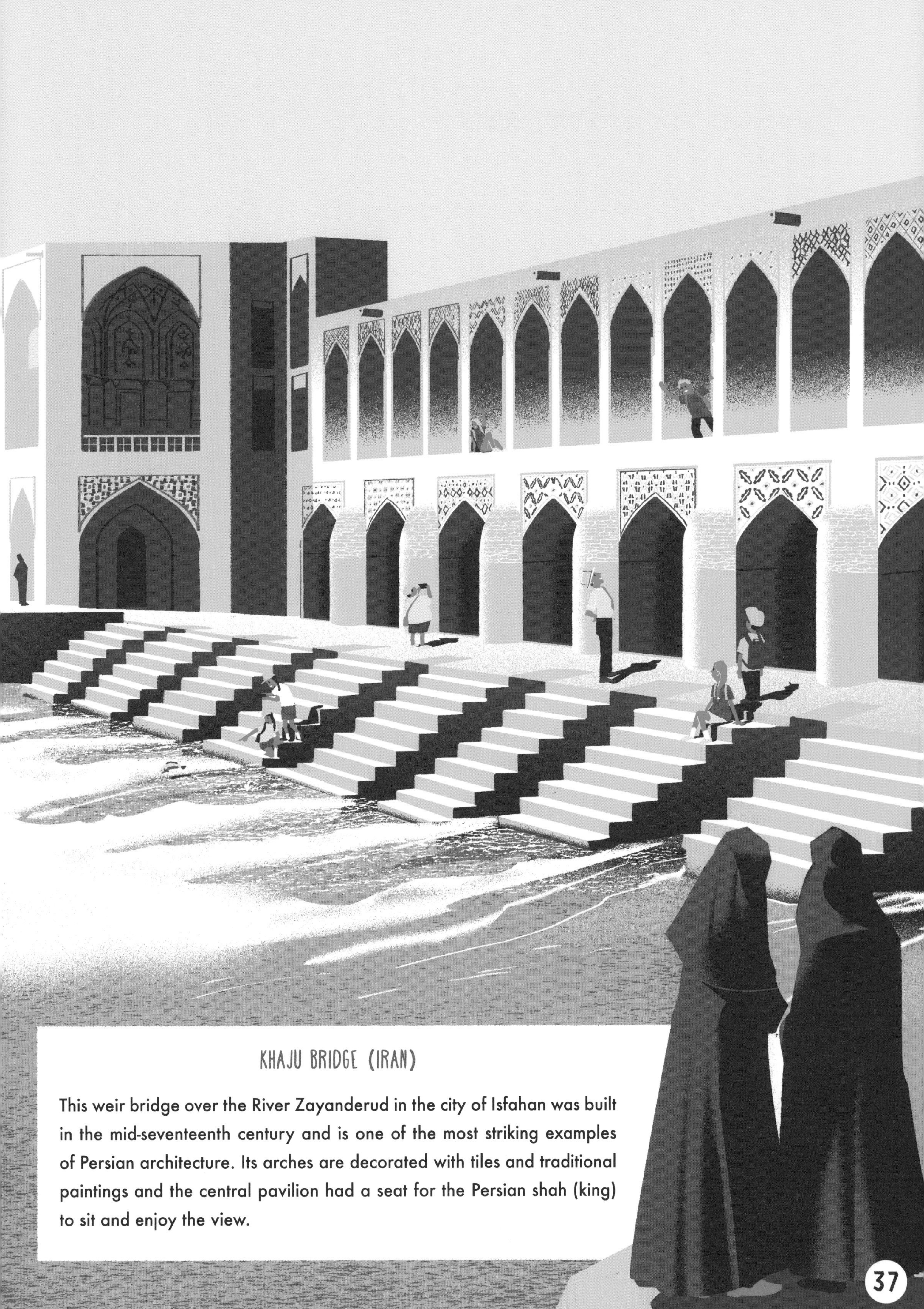

KHAJU BRIDGE (IRAN)

This weir bridge over the River Zayanderud in the city of Isfahan was built in the mid-seventeenth century and is one of the most striking examples of Persian architecture. Its arches are decorated with tiles and traditional paintings and the central pavilion had a seat for the Persian shah (king) to sit and enjoy the view.

RECORD-BREAKING BRIDGES

Since there is no standard way to design or build a bridge, all world records are a relative concept. For example, to name the tallest bridge, first we have to specify what we mean by 'height': the height of the road deck or the height of the entire structure itself, including the pylons. The height of the Millau Viaduct in France from the footings to the tip of its pylons is 343 metres (1,125 feet), making it the tallest bridge structure in the world. Meanwhile, the 269 metre (882 feet) tall Duge Bridge in China traverses a gorge so deep that the road deck is over 500 metres (1,640 feet) above the Beipan River.

The record for the longest span – the longest stretch of deck between two supports – is 1,991 metres (6,532 feet). The current record-holder is the central span of the Akashi Kaikyō Bridge, a suspension bridge in Japan. But the Danyang-Kunshan Grand Bridge, a viaduct in China, has an overall length of over 164 kilometres (101 miles)! This staggering length is made possible because it is a beam bridge. As you might recall from earlier in the book, a beam bridge can be built with any number of spans. Each span is a maximum of 80 metres (262 feet) in length. These records are sure to be broken soon by engineers using newer and stronger materials and designs.

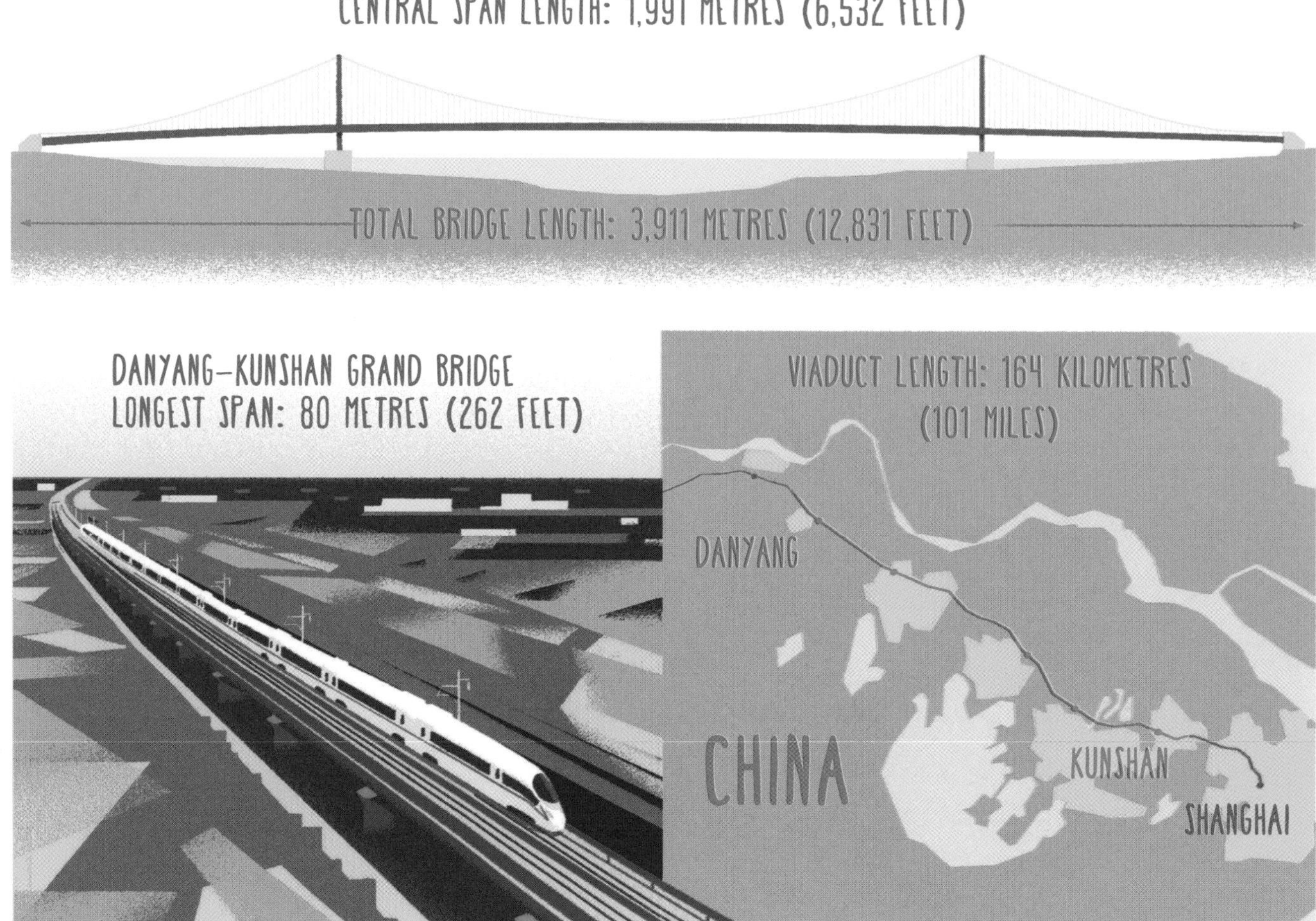

TALLEST BRIDGES

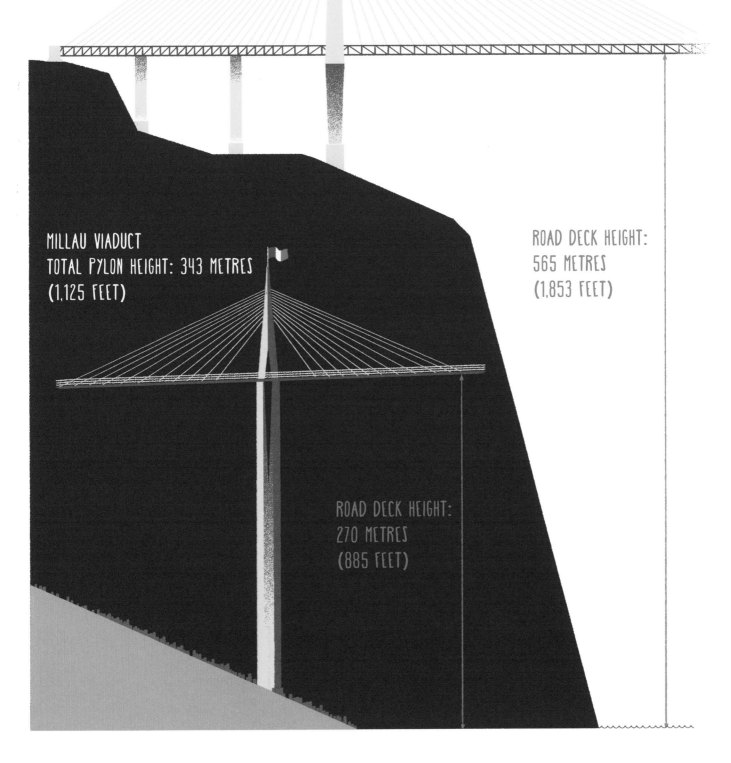

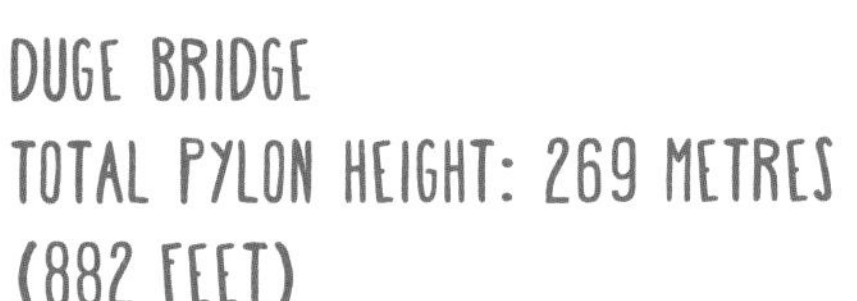

ONCE A YEAR, THE VIADUCT IS CLOSED TO TRAFFIC FOR FOUR HOURS TO BE PART OF THE ROUTE OF A MARATHON. TEN THOUSAND RUNNERS FROM AROUND THE WORLD TAKE PART.

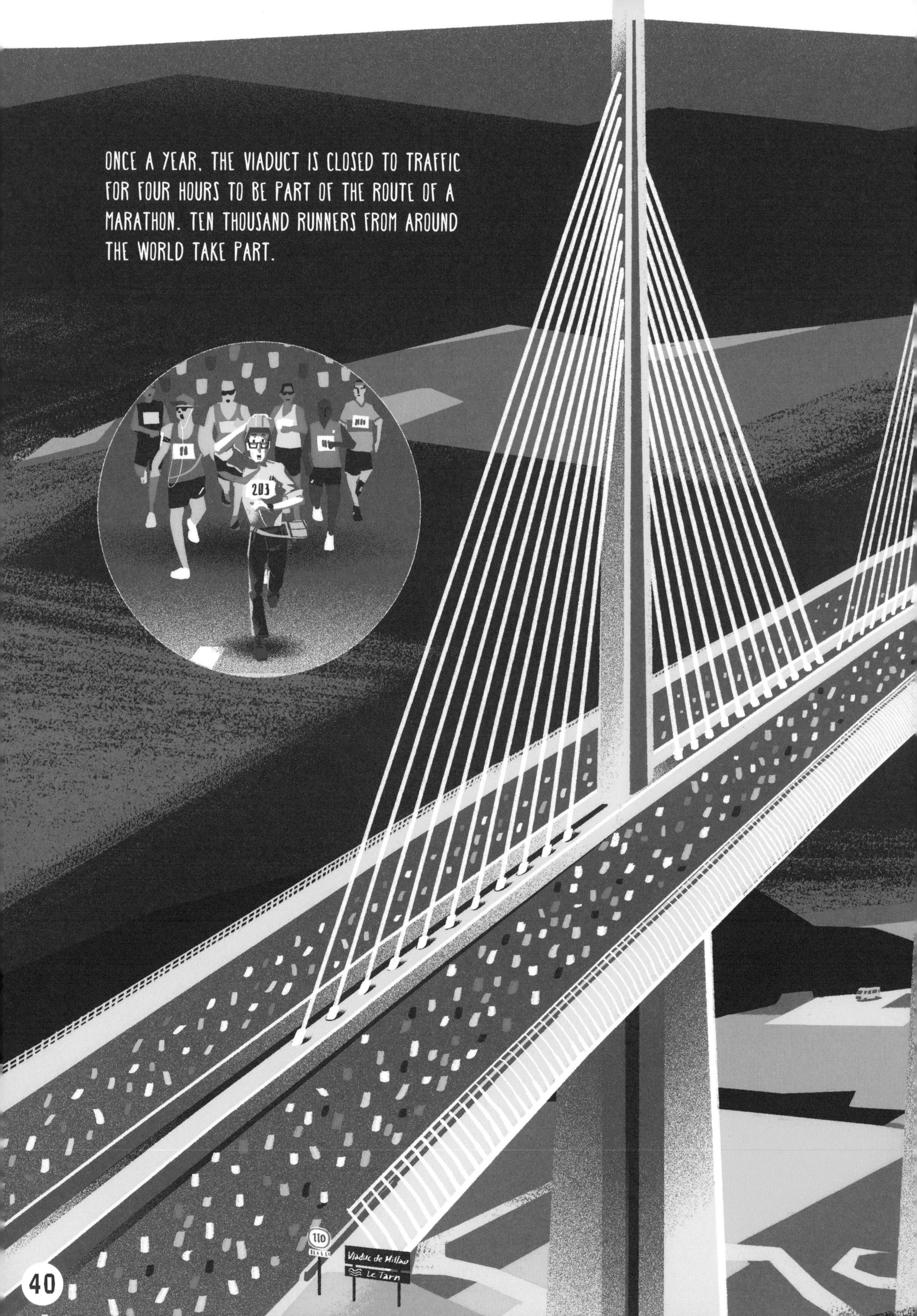

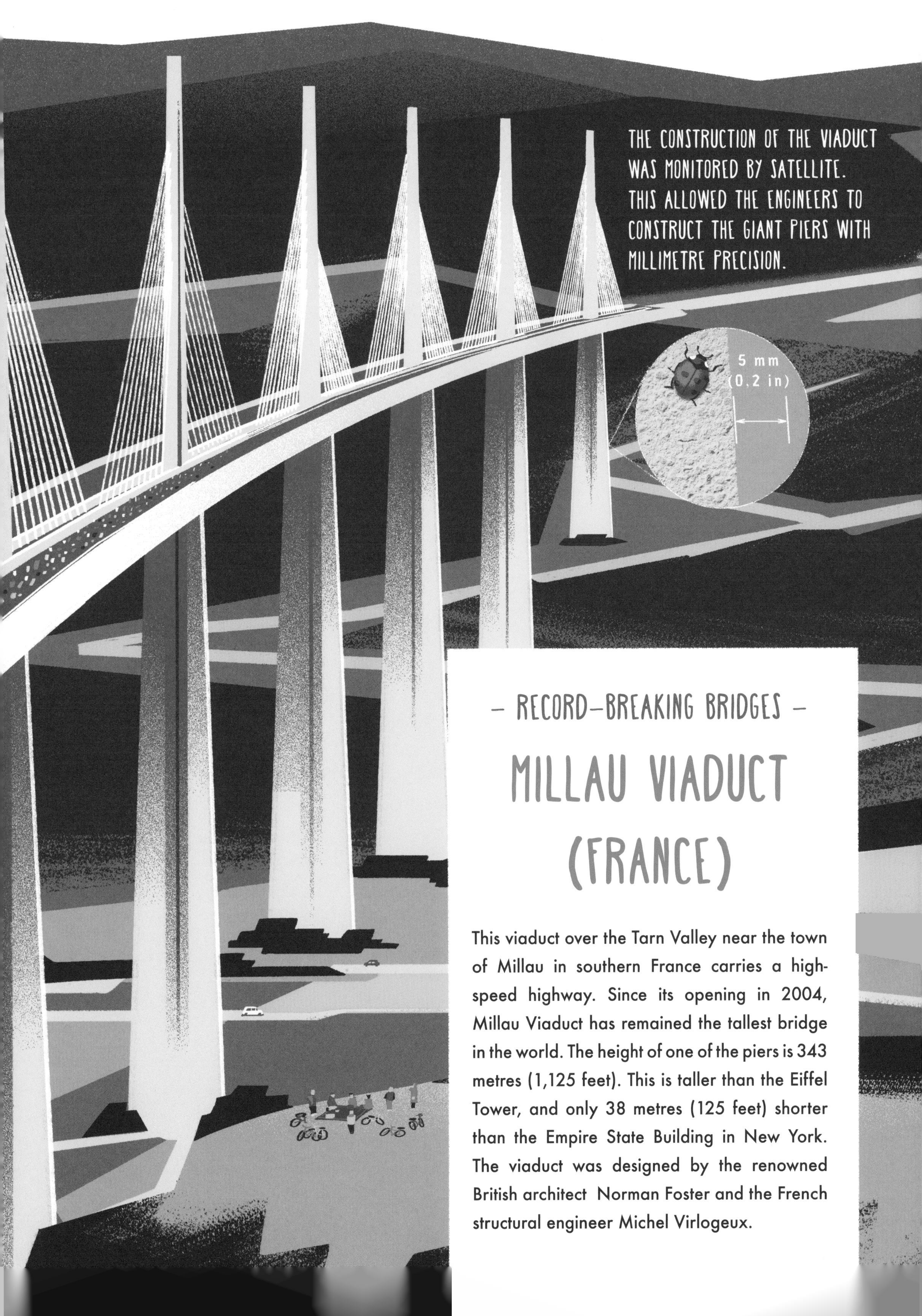

THE CONSTRUCTION OF THE VIADUCT WAS MONITORED BY SATELLITE. THIS ALLOWED THE ENGINEERS TO CONSTRUCT THE GIANT PIERS WITH MILLIMETRE PRECISION.
5 mm
(0.2 in)

– RECORD-BREAKING BRIDGES –

MILLAU VIADUCT (FRANCE)

This viaduct over the Tarn Valley near the town of Millau in southern France carries a high-speed highway. Since its opening in 2004, Millau Viaduct has remained the tallest bridge in the world. The height of one of the piers is 343 metres (1,125 feet). This is taller than the Eiffel Tower, and only 38 metres (125 feet) shorter than the Empire State Building in New York. The viaduct was designed by the renowned British architect Norman Foster and the French structural engineer Michel Virlogeux.

– RECORD-BREAKING BRIDGES –

AKASHI KAIKYŌ BRIDGE (JAPAN)

The longest span that engineers have achieved so far is the central span of the Akashi Kaikyō Bridge, at 1,991 metres (6,532 feet). This suspension bridge starts in the Japanese city of Kobe and traverses a strait to the neighbouring island. For a long time, the bridge held the world record not only for span length, but also for the height of the structure. The length of the entire bridge is 3,911 metres (12,831 feet). The bridge design was developed by engineer Satoshi Kashima and can withstand earthquakes and very strong winds.

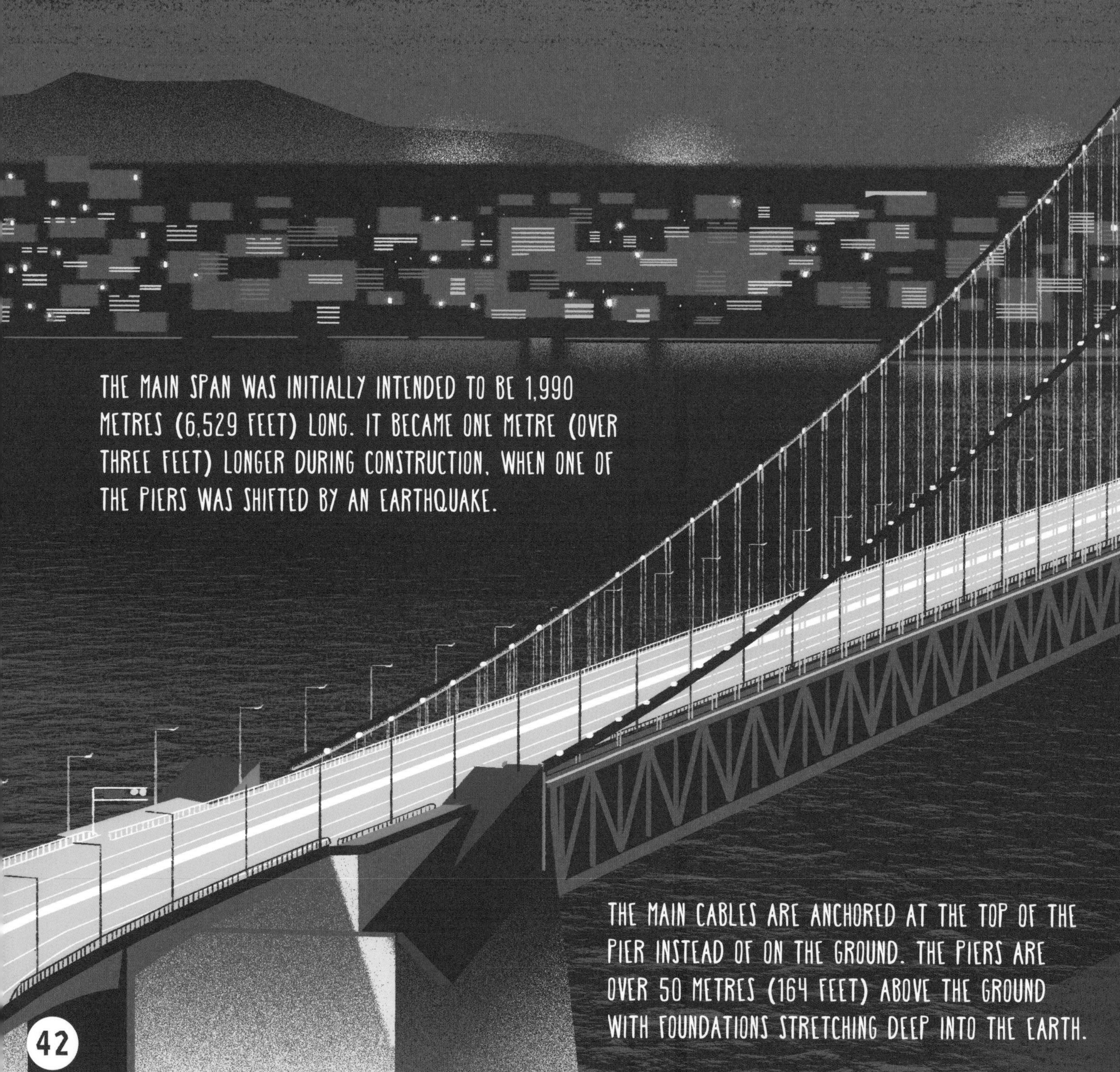

THE MAIN SPAN WAS INITIALLY INTENDED TO BE 1,990 METRES (6,529 FEET) LONG. IT BECAME ONE METRE (OVER THREE FEET) LONGER DURING CONSTRUCTION, WHEN ONE OF THE PIERS WAS SHIFTED BY AN EARTHQUAKE.

THE MAIN CABLES ARE ANCHORED AT THE TOP OF THE PIER INSTEAD OF ON THE GROUND. THE PIERS ARE OVER 50 METRES (164 FEET) ABOVE THE GROUND WITH FOUNDATIONS STRETCHING DEEP INTO THE EARTH.

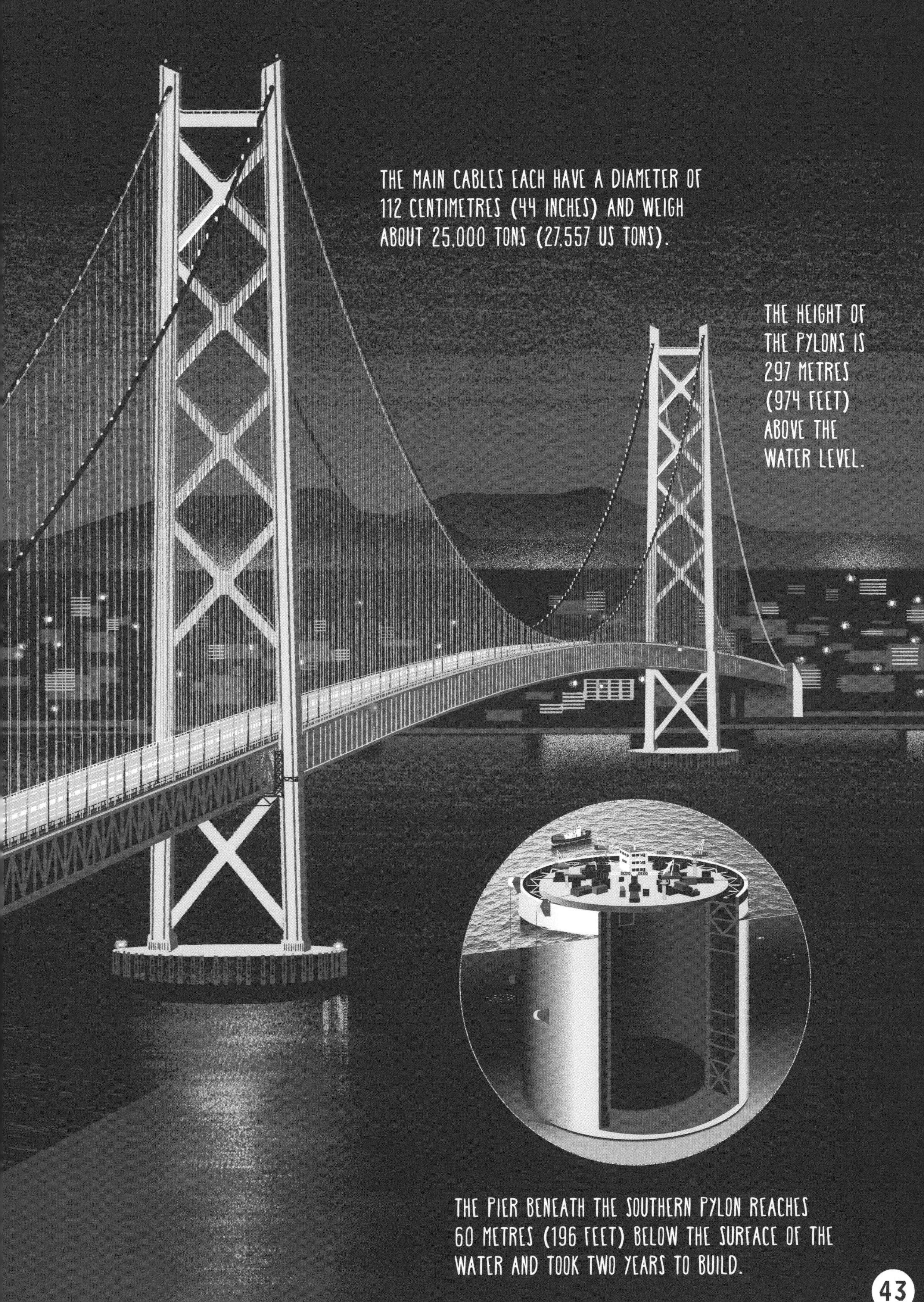
THE MAIN CABLES EACH HAVE A DIAMETER OF 112 CENTIMETRES (44 INCHES) AND WEIGH ABOUT 25,000 TONS (27,557 US TONS).
THE HEIGHT OF THE PYLONS IS 297 METRES (974 FEET) ABOVE THE WATER LEVEL.
THE PIER BENEATH THE SOUTHERN PYLON REACHES 60 METRES (196 FEET) BELOW THE SURFACE OF THE WATER AND TOOK TWO YEARS TO BUILD.

THE WESTERN FACADE OF THE BRIDGE TOWER WAS SEVERELY DAMAGED IN 1648 DURING THE SIEGE OF PRAGUE BY THE SWEDISH ARMY. A PLAQUE WAS INSTALLED BEARING THE COAT OF ARMS OF THE OLD TOWN.

PROTRUDING ICE-BREAKERS AT WATER LEVEL PROTECT THE PIERS FROM DAMAGE BY ICE FLOES.

CHARLES BRIDGE (CZECH REPUBLIC)

Charles Bridge is a famous medieval bridge over the Vltava River, connecting the two central districts of Prague, the Czech capital city. The first stone was laid in 1357 and the bridge, designed by the German-Czech architect Petr Parléř, took 45 years to build. It was some 300 years later that the 30 statues were added, one on top of each pier.

CALVARY

The first sculpture was installed in 1629 in the same spot where there had been a wooden crucifix in the fourteenth century.

ST. JOHN OF NEPOMUK

The patron saint of Prague. Legend has it that if you touch this statue, your dreams will come true.

JOHN OF MATHA AND FELIX OF VALOIS

Founders of the monastic order of the Trinitarians, whose mission was to ransom Christians from captivity.

ICONIC BRIDGES

You may not have known anything about some of the record-breaking bridges from around the world until you opened this book. But there are a few world-famous bridges that many people will recognise: they feature in movies, in tourists' selfies and on countless souvenirs. Each of these bridges is not just a marvel of structural engineering, but also a symbol of the city where it stands.

THERE IS A 31ST SCULPTURE NOT ON A MAIN PIER. IT PORTRAYS THE KNIGHT BRUNCVIK, THE CITY'S PROTECTOR. HE HOLDS A GOLDEN SWORD AND A SHIELD BEARING PRAGUE'S COAT OF ARMS.

SOUVENIRS FROM AROUND THE WORLD

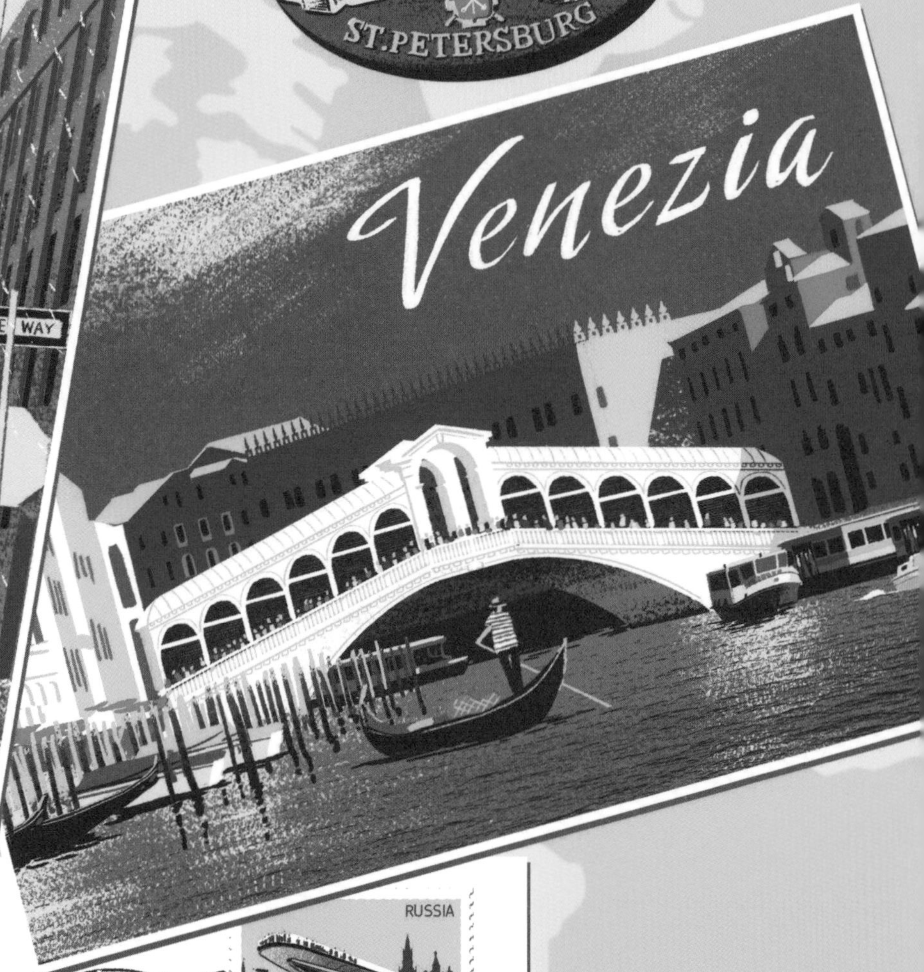

ST.PETERSBURG

Venezia

NEW YORK

ONE WAY

ROTTERDAM

RUSSIA

If you find yourself in one of the cities where these souvenirs are from, be sure to visit its famous bridge! Each of them has such an interesting story, you could write an entire book about it.

This page shows:

Manhattan Bridge
East River Strait
(New York, USA)

Palace Bridge, River Neva
(St. Petersburg, Russia)

Rialto Bridge, the Grand Canal
(Venice, Italy)

Erasmus Bridge, New Meuse River
(Rotterdam, Netherlands)

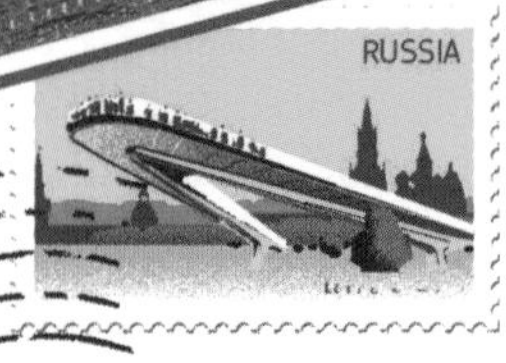

To the reader of this book!

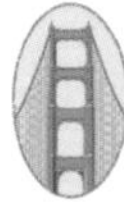

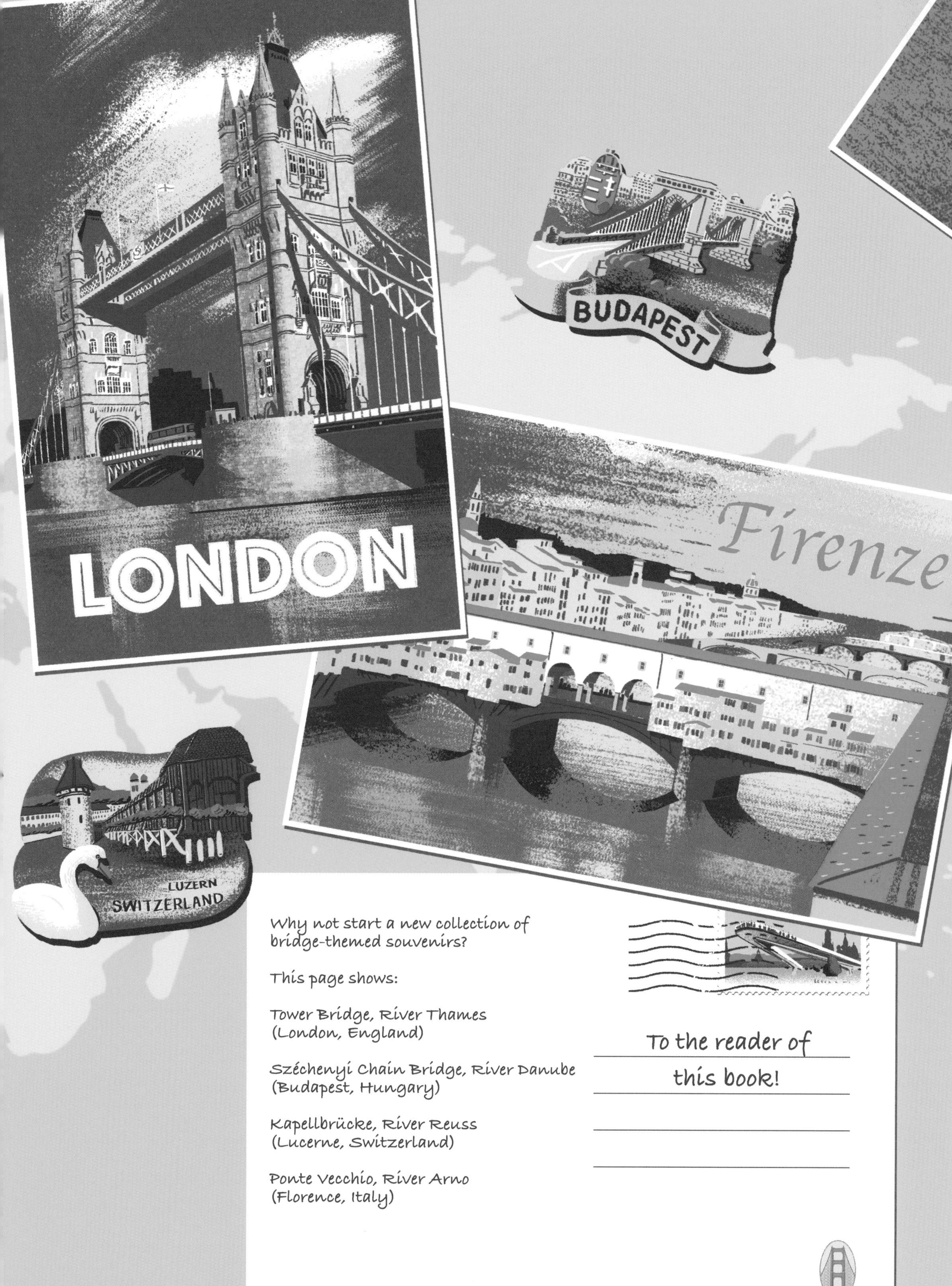

Why not start a new collection of bridge-themed souvenirs?

This page shows:

Tower Bridge, River Thames
(London, England)

Széchenyi Chain Bridge, River Danube
(Budapest, Hungary)

Kapellbrücke, River Reuss
(Lucerne, Switzerland)

Ponte Vecchio, River Arno
(Florence, Italy)

To the reader of this book!

– ICONIC BRIDGES –

SYDNEY HARBOUR BRIDGE (AUSTRALIA)

The road, rail, pedestrian and bicycle bridge over Sydney Harbour, a symbol of Australia, is one of the longest steel-arch bridges in the world. The steel structure is so huge that on hot days the 134-metre (439-foot) arch can expand by several centimetres. Six million rivets were hammered in by hand during its construction. It was designed by engineer John Bradfield and was ceremonially opened to traffic in 1932.

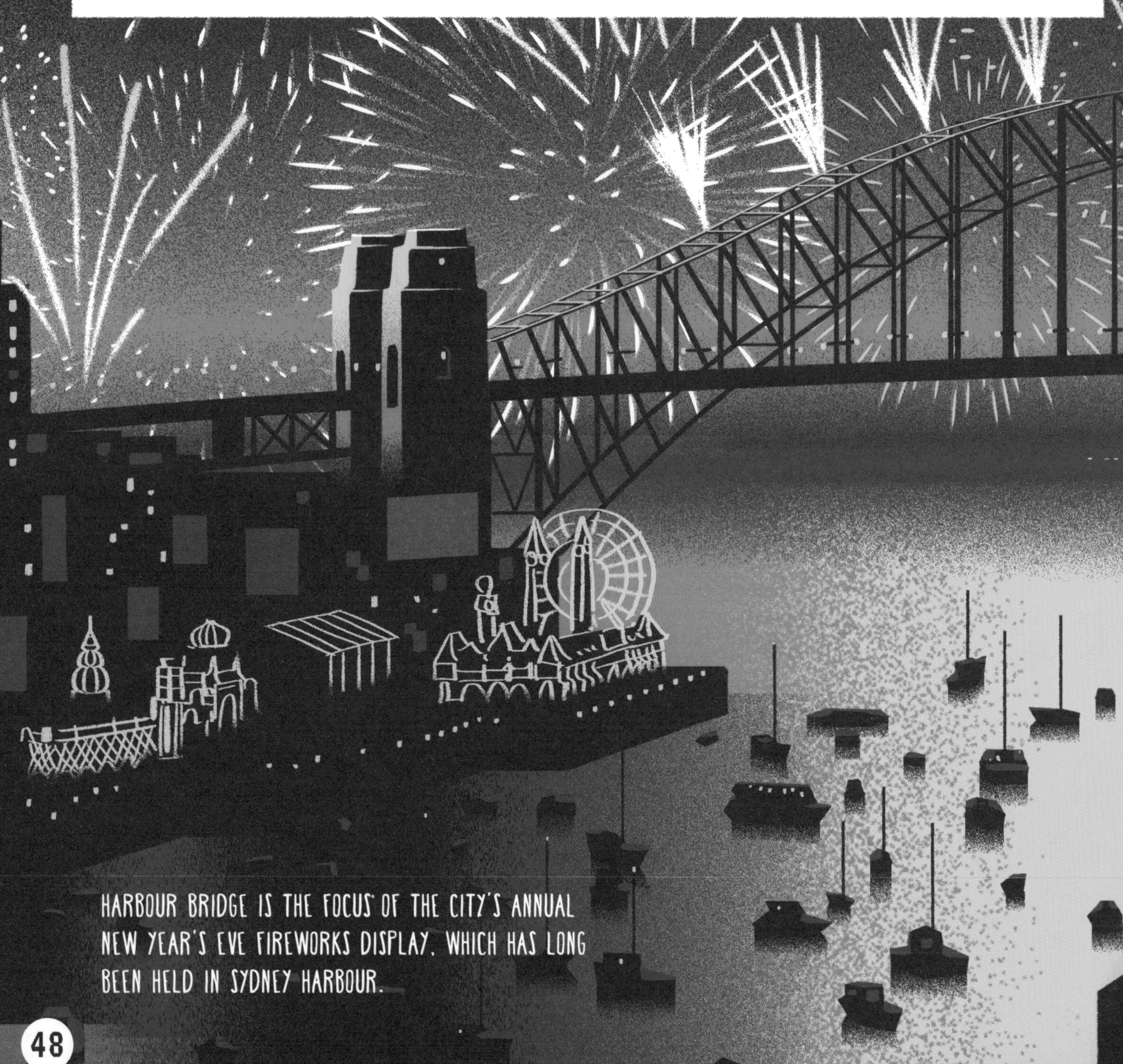

HARBOUR BRIDGE IS THE FOCUS OF THE CITY'S ANNUAL NEW YEAR'S EVE FIREWORKS DISPLAY, WHICH HAS LONG BEEN HELD IN SYDNEY HARBOUR.

— ICONIC BRIDGES —

BRIDGES ON BORDERS

Besides the Three Countries Bridge, which crosses the border between France and Germany with the border to Switzerland nearby, there are many bridges in the world that bring together countries or even entire continents. The arch bridge at Victoria Falls, the world's largest waterfall, crosses the Zambezi River at the border of the African countries of Zimbabwe and Zambia.

THE SPRAY FROM BY THE WATERFALL IS VISIBLE UP TO 50 KILOMETRES (31 MILES) AWAY.

VICTORIA FALLS BRIDGE WAS FINISHED IN 1905 AND THERE WERE PLANS FOR A TRANSCONTINENTAL AFRICAN RAILWAY TO PASS OVER IT, FROM CAIRO IN THE NORTH TO CAPE TOWN IN THE SOUTH.

Another arch bridge, the Rainbow Bridge, spans the Niagara River, which forms the border between the USA and Canada. It is a favourite vantage point for tourists who want to see Niagara Falls in all its glory.

The Øresund Bridge connects Copenhagen, the capital of Denmark, with the Swedish city of Malmö. This staggering bridge seems to tail off into the sea before reaching Denmark, as the road leads into a tunnel in an island in the open sea. The centre of the bridge is cable-stayed with a harp design.

The Bosphorus Bridge in Istanbul may not cross a national border, but its location is no less interesting. The Bosphorus is a strait separating Europe and Asia, so when you cross this suspension bridge from one part of Istanbul to the other, you can visit two continents in one day.

BRIDGES IN MYTHOLOGY

Bridges have always occupied an important place in folklore and belief. In the mythology of many cultures, the world of humans and the world of spirits were separated by an impenetrable barrier – a river of fire or a bottomless abyss – which could be traversed only via a magical bridge, inaccessible to ordinary mortals. In this section we explore some of the most famous mythical bridges between the worlds.

BIFRÖST

In Norse mythology, Bifröst is a burning rainbow bridge that connects Midgard, the world of people, and Asgard, the realm of the gods.

AS-SIRAT

In Islam, this bridge is the route for souls to cross to the afterlife. Below the Sirat burn the fires of Hell. The bridge is unimaginably long, as thin as a strand of hair and as sharp as a sword. Only those who have lived a righteous life are able to cross.

KALINOV BRIDGE

In the ancient Russian folk epics, the burning hot Kalinov Bridge spans the Smorodina River. On one side lies the realm of the living, on the other is the kingdom of the dead. To cross the Kalinov Bridge, you must first fight its guardian, a three-headed snake.

NAI HE

In Chinese mythology, souls can return from the underworld to the world of the living by crossing the Nai He bridge. Before reincarnation, the goddess Meng Po gives these souls a special tea of forgetfulness, which erases their memories of their past life.

BRIDGES IN ART

In the modern era, bridges have been a popular subject for artists and photographers. If you collected all the classical paintings depicting bridges, you would have a very impressive exhibition!

NONE OF THE BRIDGES DEPICTED ON THE EURO BANKNOTES EXIST IN REALITY. THEY ARE ALL AMALGAMATED IMAGES SYMBOLISING THE ARCHITECTURAL STYLES OF VARIOUS ERAS.

There is no need to visit an art gallery to enjoy the creativity inspired by bridges. We often have such artefacts close to hand without even noticing it. Take a closer look at the money in your wallet or piggy bank: many notes and coins from around the world feature iconic and memorable bridges.

This English language edition published by b small publishing ltd.

To order a copy or request more information, please visit our website.

www.bsmall.co.uk

Original edition first published in the Russian language by LLC "Samokat" Publishing House, 2020.

1 2 3 4 5 6 7 8 9

ISBN 978-1-911509-89-9

Translator: Ruth Ahmedzai Kemp
Publisher: Sam Hutchinson
Editorial: Catherine Bruzzone and Jenny Jacoby
Design by LLC "Samokat" Publishing House
Additional design work by Vicky Barker
Printed in Poland on FSC paper

Printed on FSC-certified papers produced from sustainable forest/controlled wood sources.

British Library Cataloguing-in-Publication Data.
A catalogue record for this book is available from the British Library.

ALSO AVAILABLE IN THE 'HOW IT WORKS' SERIES:

HOW DOES A LIGHTHOUSE WORK?

Nominated for the Kate Greenaway Award 2019
Winner of 'The Steam Children's Book Prize 2018' highlighting the importance of STEAM (Science, Technology, Engineering, Art, Maths) subjects.

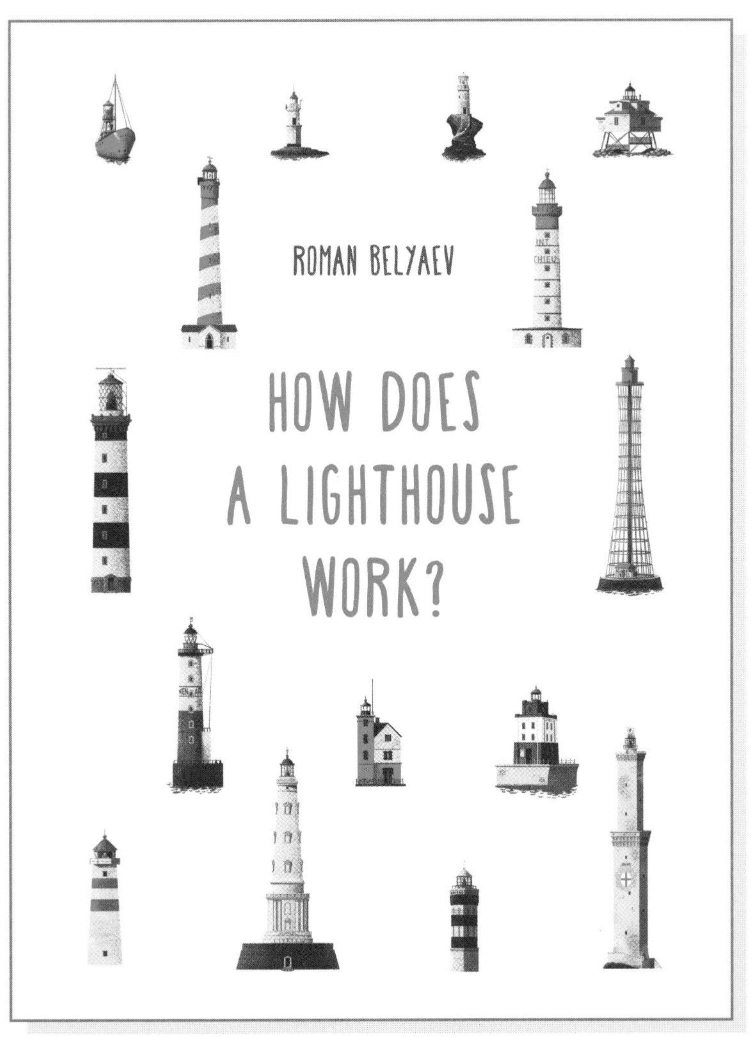

48 pages Hardback £10.99

978-1-911509-24-0

GOLDEN GATE BRIDGE

MILLAU VIADUCT

MILLENNIUM BRIDGE

FALKIRK WHEEL

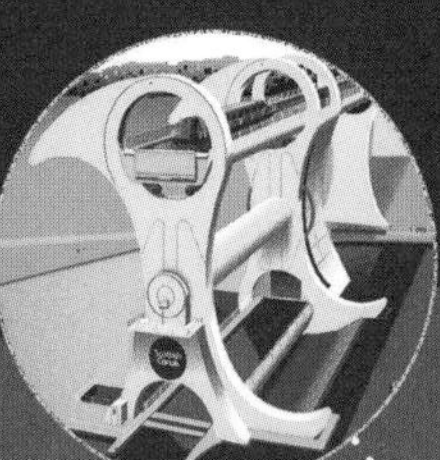

THREE COUNTRIES BRIDG

MIKE O'CALLAGHAN–PAT TILLMAN MEMORIAL BRIDGE

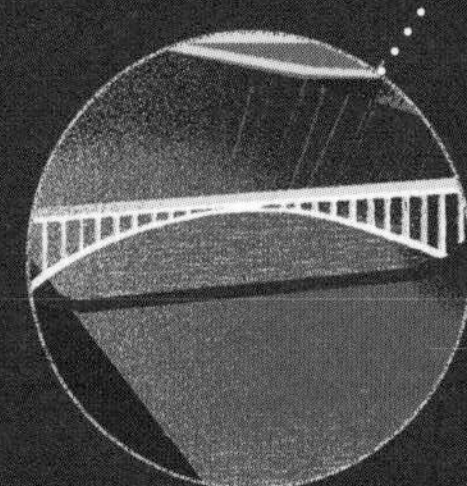

RAINBOW BRIDGE

INCA SUSPENSION BRIDGE

VIZCAYA BRIDGE

VICTOR–EMMANUEL II BRIDGE

BOSPHORUS BRIDGE